Buckskin Tanner

Books by Jaime Jackson

Equine
The Natural Horse: Lessons from the Wild (1992, rev. 2020)
Horse Owners Guide to Natural Hoof Care (1999, rev. 2002)
Founder – Prevention and Cure the Natural Way (2001)
Guide To Booting Horses for Hoof Care Professionals (2002)
Paddock Paradise: A Guide to Natural Horse Boarding (2005, rev. 2018)
The Natural Trim: Principles and Practice (2012, rev. 2019)
The Healing Angle: Nature's Gateway to the Healing Field (2014, out of print)
Laminitis: An Equine Plague of Unconscionable Proportions (2016)
the Hoof Balancer: A Unique Tool for Balancing Equine Hooves (2019)
The Natural Trim: Basic Guidelines (2019)
The Natural Trim: Advanced Guidelines (2019)
Navicular Syndrome: Healing And Prevention Using the Principles and Practices of Natural Horse Care (2021)
A Closer Approximation of ☉ On the MATW Using An Infrared Thermometer With Laser Pointer Gun (2021)

Other
Guard Your Teeth: Why the Dental Industry Fails Us – A Guide to Natural Dental Care (2018)
Buckskin Tanner: A Guide to Natural Hide Tanning (2019)
Cheyenne Tipi Notes: Technical Insights Into 19th Century Plains Indian Bison Hide Tanning (2019)
Living Behind the Facade: Memoirs Of A Gay Man's Journey Through the 20th Century (2019) by George Somers (1914-2015) with Jaime Jackson
Platform: A Humanitarian Model For An Egalitarian Society (2019)
Zoo Paradise: A New Model for Humane Zoological Gardens (2019)

Forthcoming
Horse Trek – Into the Mystic

Buckskin Tanner

A Guide to Natural Hide Tanning

Jaime Jackson

Natural World Publications

©2019 Jaime Jackson

For further information:
Natural World Publications
P.O. Box 1765
Harrison, AR 72602

Other books by the other: www.NaturalWorldPublications.com

The author may be reached at jacksonaanhcp@gmail.com

ISBN-13: 978-0-9997305-6-0

Contents

Buckskin Tanner	3
A Little Natural Tan History	10
Deer, Elk, Moose Buckskin	12
Bison Buckskin	40
Postscript	58
Chemistry of Buckskin Tanning	60
Source Material	67
Image Attributions	68
Index of Tanning Steps	69
About the author	70

To the Native American, trapper, pioneer, and all buckskin tanners of yesterday, today, and the future, the Destiny and Artful Science of Natural Tanning lies with you.
— Jaime Jackson

Buckskin Tanner

My introduction to "natural tanning" occurred in 1954 at the early age of seven, when my father took me to what was to become Disneyland in Anaheim, California. Walt Disney had brought different Indians — representing many tribes over the years — to the amusement park to help direct the building of an authentic "Indian village" as part of Frontierland. My father apparently knew several of the Indians, who somehow got us into the park before it opened to the public. I remember some of them were very old and spoke little or no English. I think after the park opened, Disney brought in Indian dance groups and also hired local Indians living in Orange County and elsewhere in Southern California who were looking for work.

My father was a traveling salesman at the time, and some of his clients were Indians living on reservations across the southwest and as far east as Oklahoma, where Disney had brought some of the Indians as I recall. My father had taken me to some of those reservations at a young age, and he shared stories about the Indians living on them. When I got older, he took me aside one day and explained that I too was part Indian. Not that that mattered to me, but what he told me otherwise was that my "dark skin" was probably going to be an issue with some people. That happened when I was 14. A girl I was interested in turned me down because, as it was explained to me by an intermediary, "you aren't a white guy." I was shocked because I always thought of myself as just another guy. As I got older, and to this day, I still get asked, "What are you?"

Anyway, Disney technicians procured commercially tanned animal hides and the Indians told them what to do with them, including how to make the teepees. There was some discussion about how Indians tanned hides with my father, to which I was an attentive listener. But no "Indian tanning" took place there as I recall. The entire village was dismantled years later, and I learned from Disney staff in the 1970s that all the hide teepees were destroyed in 1961, including the one at the front of this chapter.

Years later, as a young man, my interest in Indian tanning was reawakened after coming across a book on the subject, *Tanning the Sioux Way*, by Larry Belitz. We began to communicate, and I eventually learned a lot from Larry, a school teacher who taught at the Pine Ridge Indian Reservation at the time (early 1970s), until forced to leave due to violence occurring there related to the infamous Wounded Knee incident in 1973. Larry's uncle, I recall him saying, was an Indian reservation agent, and I believe he had some influence in Larry's own developing interest in Native American culture. Larry became a technical advisor for the movie "Dances With Wolves and other films where historical representation of tribal culture was important. He himself learned things from elder Sioux women, including Flossie Bear Robe, who taught him traditional bead and porcupine quill embroidery, Sioux designs, and other things. Much of this I learned from Larry with input from Flossie, whom Larry quoted in a letter to me years ago, "Jaime's work is too perfect for the Sioux!" *Sigh*. She passed away in 1988 at age 66, in the hamlet of Oglala near the Pine Ridge Indian Reservation.

During the mid-1970s I had ventured into a two year, solo horseback ride across the Deep South (*facing page*). To support myself during that trek, I tanned many deer, moose and elk skins for Larry, and also prepared a number of buffalo (bison) bull hides for traditional shield making. Besides all of this tanning, I did quite a bit of quill and beadwork, all of which ended up in the hands of different collectors, including Larry.[1] I also made buffalo coats, buckskin shirts, knife sheaths, gloves, moccasins, and other

---

[1] To my shocking surprise, 40 plus years later I saw on the Internet that Larry was being sued by a South Dakota physician for $421,000 for selling him "bogus artifacts that supposedly belonged to Crazy Horse, Sitting Bull, Red Cloud and other Native American heroes." I hope my stuff wasn't part of the goods! [See: https://news.artnet.com/art-world/south-dakota-ccollector-claims-421k-fake-indian-art-390452} Then, if that wasn't enough, in late 2017 Larry and 30 others were charged with violations of the Bald and Golden Eagle Protection Act, Migratory Bird Treaty Act, and Lacey Act. According to federal prosecutors, this had to do with the "black market for eagle carcasses, feathers and other parts, which are often used in Native American-style handicrafts. Federal law limits possession of eagle feathers and other parts to enrolled members of federally recognized tribes who use them in religious practices." All of this is news to me — Larry was always straight-up with me, paying me for my work, shipping hides wherever I had set up camp, sharing what he knew about traditional Indian crafts. I'm not sure whatever came of his case, but he was always a good guy to me. [See: https://www.kotatv.com/content/news/Feds-indict-16-more-defendants-SD-eagle-black-market-case-448688333.html]

(*Top*) Me outfitted with "brain tanned" buckskin during my 2 year horse trek in the 1970s. That's "Brandy," who covered a thousand miles with me. (*Below*) Bison robe (coat) I made for a fellow whom I met during the horse trek.

things for people I met along the way. I even wore a buckskin shirt I made from deerskins I tanned somewhere along the horseback journey. The buffalo hide work on one occasion makes for an interesting story . . .

I was camped along a bayou, a slow moving river in southern Alabama, early on in the trek. I was traveling with two horses at the time, a pinto and Appaloosa. Larry had shipped two buffalo hides for me to work on. They were huge and required lacing frames 18 by 20 ft, which I fashioned from Pine saplings I gathered in the remote surrounding forest. To deflesh them, I first soaked the hides while strung in the frames, which I had laid in the river. Two ropes were secured to the corners of the frame, then up and over a long overhanging branch of a massive tree. I picked this tanning site because of that tree. I tied these ropes to the riding and pack saddles of my two horses, who then pulled and raised the hides out of the water. Saturated and weighed down with water, it would have been impossible for me to do it alone. An enormous "waterfall" flowed down from the hides! The frames were then secured tightly against the branch.

All of this commotion attracted the attention of numerous alligators in the bayou, who had gathered to watch! What a spectacle! While I suppose they could have lunged ashore at me and the horses, they didn't, and seemed only curious enough to observe with eyes and snouts just above the waterline. Later, when the hides were lowered back into the water, the alligators would bump the frames with their long snouts, no doubt attracted to the smell of the hides. But they never attacked the frames with open mouths and seemed satisfied to just watch me work. During the defleshing phase of the process (all of which I'll explain later in the tanning method), I stood upon a makeshift scaffold I created about five feet above the shoreline. I looked down below me to see several alligators snapping up the droppings! That was a bit unnerving, to say the least. But as I finished, they retreated back into the river as though on cue. They never approached me as I worked the lower half of the hides. For the two weeks in the forest campsite, these animals came daily to watch me work — but never once displayed aggression towards me or the horses. Interesting, I had many

Drawing by George Catlin (July 26, 1796 - December 23, 1872) was an American painter, author, and traveler, who specialized in portraits of Native Americans during the 1830s. Of this scene, Catlin wrote: " . . . but a small portion of the village is shown . . . as the wigwams as well as the customs, are the same in every part of it. In the foreground . . . is seen women "graining" buffalo robes."

encounters with wildlife on the journey that one would think would have been life-threatening, but weren't. That and other experiences are going into my biography about the horse trek.

Over the years I also had the opportunity to share tanning information with North American Native Americans. What I learned is that everyone seems to have their own method, often held "secretly." No different, I have my own method that evolved from seeing what others have done and adapting to what I think works best for me. A certain amount has come from historical accounts, but invariably those were written by observers, not the tanners themselves, and they clearly missed a lot of what's actually involved. One notable exception was the early 20th century anthropologist and ethnographer James Mooney.

Mooney convinced Southern Cheyenne and Arapho living in Oklahoma to tan cow hides for posterity sake and then have them use those hides to make a tipi. Doing research on Native American Indian tanning, I came across his notes on what the Indians did. I will say this, they were

Sioux (Dakota) woman graining bison hide.

wonderfully detailed, but nearly impossible to read. Mooney's lousy handwriting was legend in his time among other anthropologists, including bureaucrats at the Smithsonian's Bureau of Ethnology, who funded his research with considerable frustration — imploring him to spend more time "translating" his field notes, and less time in the field! It took me months to transcribe them into something readable, but more importantly, insightful into 19th century bison tanning by Plains Indians, and particularly useful to buckskin tanners like myself. I've dedicated an entire chapter to that tipi and the tanning that took place, including some surprising facts about buffalo tanning in general. If you're a tanner already, and you've struggled with tanning buffalo hides, then this information should prove very useful to you. It certainly did to me.

I've been asked more than once to teach others how to tan. Well, I have done that. On several occassions I have given tanning clinics, wherein everyone got to tan their own hides. The last one I gave was 20 years ago, so it's something that doesn't really motivate me anymore. This book may have to suffice. By the way, to date I've tanned over 700 hides. I decided to write this book as though you are with me and I'm showing you what I do. In fact, you're going to help me along the way, because having two people doing it together is much easier than doing it alone. Don't worry, we won't be doing this near any alligators! In fact, we'll do it as though in the privacy of your own backyard. If your fence isn't high enough, you may have to have a talk with your neighbors first. Hopefully, they'll be interested enough to come watch! If you live on a ranch, then no problem. So that you know, no harmful chemicals are used, so there's no pollution to be concerned about.

Read on!

A Little Natural Tan History

As it turns out, "natural tanning," as I've come to think of it, isn't indigenous to just American Indians of long ago or today, for that matter. It seems that just about all pre-industrialized peoples more or less did the same thing. Modern chemical tanning didn't arrive until well into the Industrial Revolution of the 19th and 20th centuries. With its arrival, people everywhere pretty much gave up tanning on their own. Like today, they simply went to the store to buy leather shoes, purses, wallets and so forth. Tanning was as much an "untidy" affair as it was tedious and time-consuming. Nevertheless, "ancient" natural tanning has always been of interest to many people in the modern age, including myself. We do it because it is fascinating. Often it fits into social organizations we may be involved with, where "old time" leather is part of their gig, such as the many buckskinner associations around the world today. Such leather also shows up as a part of historical reenactments of the old 18th century fur trade, pioneer life in the Old West, mountain men, American Indians, traders, and even tanners! I've never personally been involved with any of them, though I've made things for some of their members. Like the buffalo coat in the previous chapter that I put together for a fellow from New Jersey 40 years ago or so. I can't recall for sure, but I think he stumbled upon me during my horseback trek years, or just after. He probably thought I was crazy, but I was doing things for real to survive at the time, that lot of those "reinactors" do for fun!

I thought about including a history of "primitive tanning," as natural tanning is often called, but I decided against it. Instead I've included a fairly extensive bibliography that I thoroughly gleaned during the early years of my learning for useful information. Most of it is about Indian tanning over a century ago. It doesn't take long before you realize that the writers who were first hand observers, weren't tanners themselves. If you've tanned successfully yourself, you'll see this. At times, the "observed" are humorous, playfully pulling the wool over the eyes of their gullible visitors to make fun. But at other times genuinely offering themselves as informants about an important feature of their culture.

When I could, I sourced material about native tanning where specimens were available for inspection, namely in museums. This really was necessary because it was painfully clear to me that first hand accounts of 19th century Indian tanning, for example, often made no sense or were so rudimentary and missing such important steps as to be completely useless. I found this to be particularly true of bison hide tanning. Even today, things written by contemporary natural tanners simply don't add up to what was historically happening among Indian tanners. Most natural tanners today are familiar with "brain tanning." Claims have been made that one can tan deer and bison hides with brains. In fact, it isn't possible, and it never happened — contrary to popular belief today — in any Indian camp, or anywhere else, for that matter. Animal brains are chemically or otherwise unable to tan anything. Stated simply, "brain tanning" is a myth. This statement is going to anger brain tan proponents, but tanning science I'll be discussing before this book is finished is going to save my reputation, if not my neck.

I suppose, then, this is the perfect place to define what tanning is. *It is the process of treating skins and hides of animals to produce leather.* The word "hide" is related to the German word "haut" which means skin. So the terms skin and hide really mean the same thing. In this book, I use them interchangeably without rhyme nor reason. Everyone knows what leather is, so we need not go into that, except to say that commercially produced leather varies as much in look and feel as are the tanning chemicals and methods deployed to create them. Natural tanning is more limited: hair (or fur)-on or removed. *Grain leather* refers to the outer side of a hide, called the epidermis, where the hair grows out of. *Suede leather* is the result of removing the grain layer from the hide. Natural tanning typically removes the grain, thus is a type of suede leather, called "buckskin" — unless one wants the hair left intact, the product then called a *fur* or *robe*. The well-known buffalo robe is such an example.

Having said this, I will leave the reader to do what I did — study the history of native tanning and become informed. The reading is interesting, but ultimately, from the standpoint of understanding the nuances of natural tanning, at times tediously repetitive, frustrating and disappointing. On a brighter note, the following chapters do describe in detail how to tan the "natural way," including members of the bovine family — like the buffalo.

Deer, Elk, Moose Buckskin

Insofar as natural tanning goes, I take the narrowest definition possible for buckskin. Buckskin is leather typically made from the deer family (Cervidae). Here in North America, this includes the common deer, elk, and moose. But, as you'll learn in the next chapter, we can also make buckskin from bison hide. Buckskin, we recall, is suede leather, and if you leave the hair on, then it's fur (or robe), not buckskin. Deer hair is hollow and sharp to the feel, so it is typically removed. We're going to remove it. Because we want buckskin.

My manner of buckskinning evolved from my propensity to be pragmatic, efficient, and neat and clean as possible. I don't like stinky, gooey or rotting messes. We're not going to have that. We don't want the neighbors complaining do we? I also don't like unnecessary labor. One reads in the historical texts about the "labor intensive" method. Well that's all pretty relative. What I find is that if one is orderly about this, there's probably no more work, probably less, than what they do in the commercial tanneries. Industrialized hides go through a lot, and they're very polluting. We don't pollute. And, in my opinion, buckskin is better leather: stronger, cleaner, and as beautiful, if not more so, than anything coming out of those polluting plants. But you'll have to decide that for yourself.

There are identifiable "steps" involved. Actually, they are processes that necessarily follow in a certain order if quality buckskin is our objective. I won't assume you know anything about animal skins (tanned or untanned). The main steps are pretty straight forward: remove the hair, remove the flesh, remove the grain, and then tan what's left over. Pretty simple, eh? Not so fast! It's the nuance involved in each step that will make you successful at this, or a failure. I'm not interested in failure, so give this book to someone else if you don't want to be a winner. Go buy your buckskin.

There are different ways to remove the hair. I prefer the easiest, and that's what we're going to do together. Whether we're going to do a deer, elk, or moose, the hair comes off the same way. By the way, I have to assume you've been smart enough to preserve your deer skin by either freezing it inside a plastic bag, or you've got it salted down real good. Just in case, here's how you salt the hide to preserve it until ready for tanning:

Salt the hide

Get some rock salt from the feed store in a 25-lb. sack if you can, 50 if they have it, because I'm hoping you'll want to do more than one skin by the time I'm done with you. Find an old plywood board big enough to fit the entire skin. Cover the plywood with a sheet of Visqueen plastic. You want a half inch thick layer of the salt under the skin, so figure that out. Lay the skin down on the salt, flesh side up, hair side down facing the salt. Then cover the flesh side with salt. Really lay it on thick (like an inch thick). Make sure you're doing this where dogs or other critters can't get at it, or it will be gone or torn to shreds by tomorrow morning. Leave it over night covered in the salt.

The next day add more salt if the layer you previously put on has drawn fluids (mainly blood) to the surface. Which is typical. Put another layer of salt under the skin, then add another inch thick layer on top. Give it another overnight. If it's still drawing liquid the next morning, add more layers of salt. Usually by the third day the fluids are drawn out. When this happens, shake most of the salt off and roll the skin up and store it away from the critters. You might want to put it in a large burlap bag, out of the sunlight, and store it in a shed. It can keep like this for years. Having said all this, wouldn't it be easier to just freeze the skin unsalted in a freezer? A small freezer you can keep in the shed just for your hides?

Now back to the hair removal.

Remove the hair

There are different ways to remove the hair. Some tanners let the hide dry on a frame or staked on the ground, and then scrape it off. They call that the "dry scrape" method. Others scrape it off while the hide is wet. You guessed it, they call it "wet scrape." Both are a pain in the ass, so I don't do either, though I tried them both, "just in case." Here's what I do:

Go back to the feed store, or garden nursery, or hardware store, or wherever, and get a sack of hydrated garden lime. While you're there, get a 35 gallon plastic trash can with a lid. Notice I've got you doing all the work so far. I like that. Now head back home.

Fill the plastic trash can half full with water straight out of the garden hose.

Examples of dry scrape de-hairing a deer hide (*left*) and wet scrape de-hairing and defleshing a bison hide over a beam (*right*). I was teaching these methods here to naturalists years ago at Coyote Hills Regional Park (Hayward, California) because they wanted to know. But were not going to do this to any hide in my method.

Put the frozen, or salted, hide in the water. Let it soak in there over night. Not so fast! You'll notice that it's probably floating in there. This is due to the hollow hair and any air trapped in the folds of the skin. That's not going to work, because anything sticking up above the waterline will dry out and become or stay rawhide. We don't want rawhide, we want buckskin. Find something to hold it down under. I've even used a heavy enough rock. You're clever, though, and will figure this one out. Whatever you use, make sure it doesn't have rust or some kind of dye or something that's going to penetrate and blemish the skin. Or you may end up with some weird kind of tie-dyed piece of leather that all the hippies down on the ol' commune will want to use. By the way, if you haven't figured out yet that you should be wearing a sturdy pair of rubberized gloves, the time has come to return to the hardware store get a couple of pairs. While you're getting all that together, I'm heading to the house. The hide needs to soak submerged all night. I'll see you in the morning.

Next day

The frozen hide will be defrosted by now. The salted hide will be ready too, but you'll need to dump the liquid and soak him again several times, with changes of water. You can do this in ten or fifteen minutes. Once the water is clear of salt (and maybe some blood) and runs clear, you're ready to move on. Ditto the same for the frozen hide if the water isn't clear either.

Return the hide to the trash barrel. Add maybe a fourth of the barrel with fresh water, just enough water to cover the hide when it's held down. Now add a half a gallon or so of the lime. You want to add enough lime that the water is milky looking. With a stick, slosh the hide around in this lime bath until the lime's all dissolved. Weight the hide down again, and leave it in there over night.

Next day

Wearing your gloves, pull the hide out of the lime bath and drape it over the side of the trash barrel. Tug at the hair with your gloved fingers. If the hairs don't slip off real easy, or at all, submerge the hide again, and leave it overnight once more. See you in the morning.

Next day

Repeat everything you did on day 2. If the hair doesn't slip off, repeat this step again. Some hides are resistant to let their hair go. But most will give it up in 3 to 5 days, some sooner. What's happening here is the lime has created an alkaline solution ("high pH") which causes the hide to swell (it actually thickens and shrinks overall a bit) and its hair follicles ("pores") to open up and release the hair. Once it does it, the hair comes off easily. Just swipe all of it off with your gloved hand. Okay, you've got your marching orders. Get all the hair slipped off and then let's move on again. The next step is pretty interesting, and I'm dying to get to it.

De-lime the hide

Now that all the hair has been brushed off, it's time to shrink the swollen hide back down to its normal thickness and close the follicles so we can get the show on the road. So, it's back to the garden nursery for you to pick up a small box of *aluminum sulphate*,[1] used for making soil less acidic (lowers the pH, which is what we want to do now). Once you've got it, dump out the lime bath (you can

---

[1] You can also use white vinegar, but I prefer the aluminum sulphate for its reactivity with the alkaline lime bath.

dump all our tanning solutions right on the grass somewhere – they don't pollute anything. In fact, all these ingredients are used by gardeners and farmers. They're safe and biodegrade readily. Next, put the hide back in the barrel and add just enough water to cover it. Add in a cup of the aluminum sulphate and stir it all around, saturating the hide. Leave it in the solution overnight.

Next day

Check the hide in the morning. It will have shrunk down to its natural thickness. Dump out the solution, and rinse the hide in clear water. Dump that solution too.

Make your stretching frame

This step really brings us closer to the "pre-tan" phase of the tanning process. That means getting the brains worked into the raw skin. But first, we have to prepare the skin to receive the brains. This means making a "stretching frame," a common centerpiece of natural tanning down through the centuries.

As you've probably seen it coming, you've got another trip to the hardware store to make the frame. We're talking about a shopping list, and here it is: you'll need five 8 ft. 2 x 4s, several pounds of 1 to 1½ in. fencing staples, eight 4 in. x ¼ in. plated lag screws (for securing the corner braces, and you'll need a socket wrench, drill and bit to do this), and eight 25 ft. lengths of $3/16$ in. braided nylon rope.[1] If you don't have a table saw, or aren't really handy with a hand saw, do what I do and have one of the fellows down at Home Depot or Lowes cut the boards, particularly the corner braces, for you.

I've drawn a buckskin tanning frame like I use (*facing page*), and you'll see photos of mine (and variations) in use throughout these instructions. Let the drawing serve as your template, and replicate it the best you can. Use common nails or wood screws to join the 2 x 4 lengths. The corner braces will serve to really clamp things together tightly. You'll need a hammer to set the staples in the 2 x 4s; I position these 2 to 3 in. apart all around the frame on one side only.

Following these directions makes for a very sturdy frame that will not bend or twist when hides are mounted, stretched, dried, and worked vigorously. Once you've got the frame put together, I'll meet you at the next step. Do a good job,

---

[1] Walmart sells these for clothesline ropes as polypropylene blends in 50 foot lengths for under 2^{00}. Cut these in half and heat seal the frayed ends.

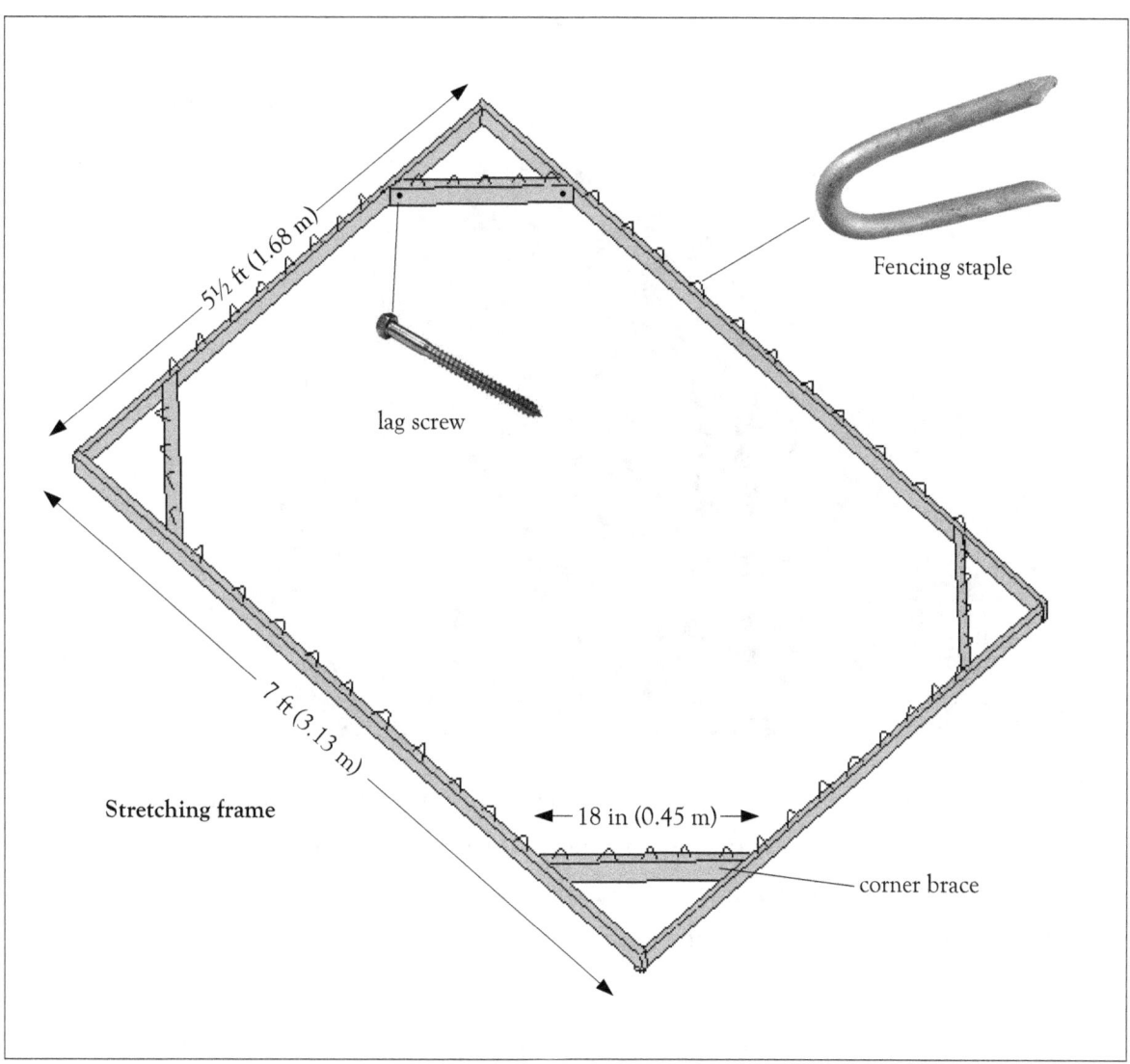

because you'll be using that frame a lot.

Make your scraping tool

Unless you want to use your fingernails and teeth in the next step, which I don't really recommend, you'll need to make your scraping tool. Mine is the most effective type you can use, in my opinion, and it will out live you — not a pleasant thought. But it's true. You can pass it along to your son or daughter to use after your gone. But I don't think that's going to happen because they're all interested in computer games, Facebook, and other social media. I call them the "lost generation." God help them.

My scraping tool is made from an automobile leaf spring. It holds a sharp edge very well, and its weight is ideal for working the hide. You can get one at a

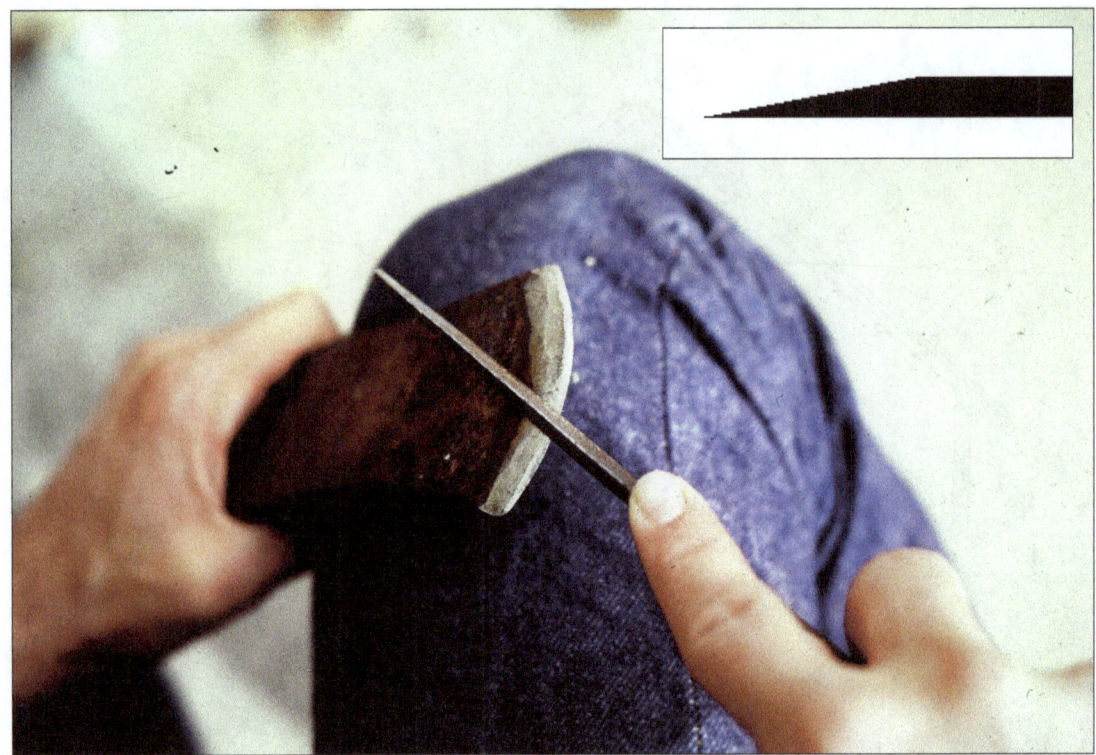

local wrecking yard for next to nothing. Maybe for nothing. You can see me using one in most any of the accompanying photos. I've had several over the years because I've always been on the move, one step away from being a nomad. Mine have been about two inches wide (not too wide, or it won't fit comfortably in your hands), and 1½ to 2 feet long.

One end (the sharpened end) is initially ground down and sharpened on a bench grinder, creating a wide bevel. If you have a forge, you can hammer out the bevel, but this isn't really necessary. The cutting edge formed is then fine finished with a metal file (*above*), creating a slightly sharper, secondary edge. This secondary cutting edge needs to be kept very sharp; so, the initial bevel on the grinder needs to be more flat than acute (*inset, above*), "zero degree." Otherwise it's virtually impossible to get a sharp enough edge to do what we need to do to the hide. The corners of the cutting edge should be slightly rounded so they won't readily puncture the hide.

Okay, with that out of the way, it's back to the stretching frame.

Lace the hide onto your frame

Lay the frame down on some grass or even on a clean slab of concrete — but

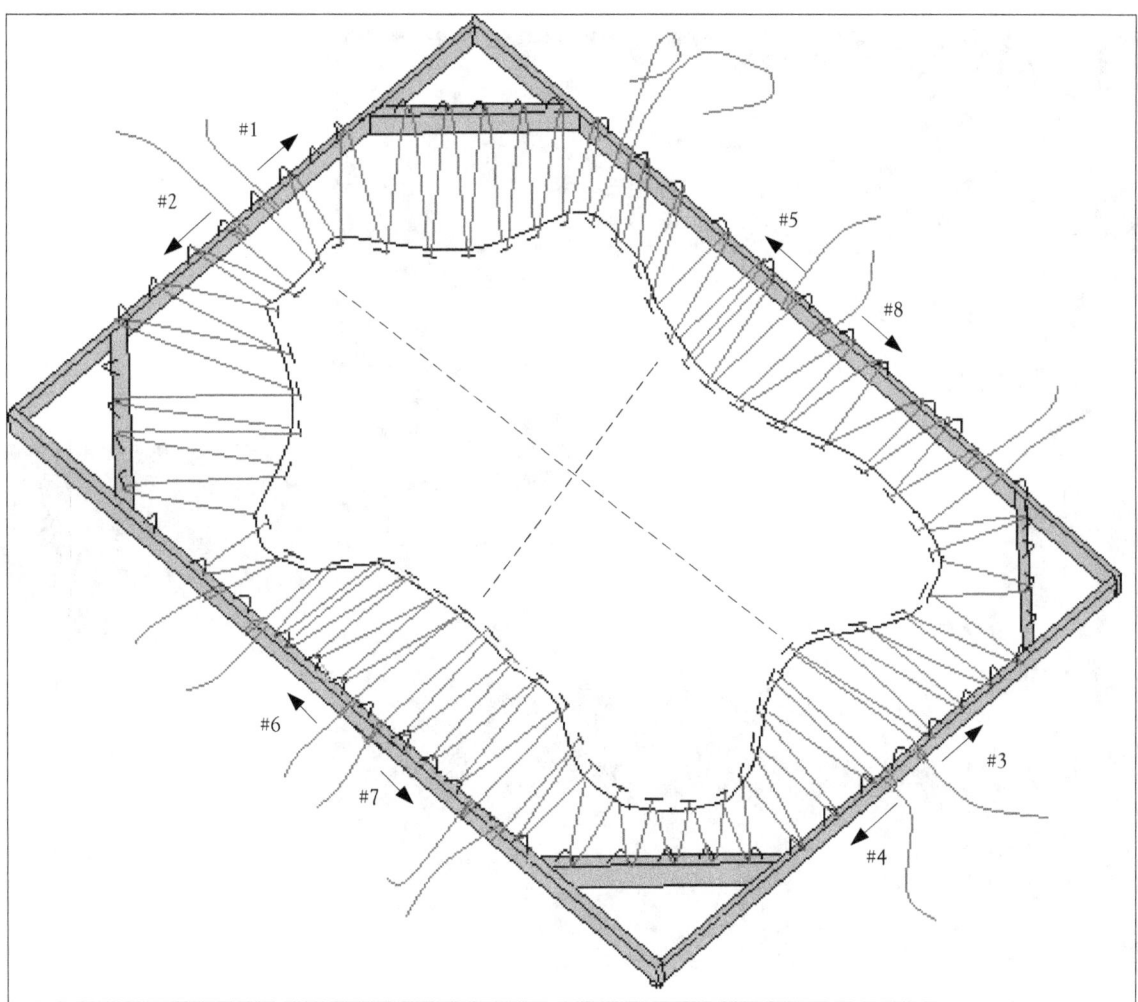

not on dirt or on a tar driveway. Open the hide, flesh side up, and center it within the frame (*above*). Slice one inch slits all around the perimeter of the hide, 3 to 4 inches apart. Go in about an inch from the outer edge. Get too close and the slit might tear open. You'll need a sharp hunter's knife to do this work.

Next, lace the hide to the frame. You'll need two 25 ft. rope bundles per hide quadrant, a total of 8 bundles, each 25 ft. long. Start at the neck of the hide and go in both directions (*above*, #1 and #2) towards the sides of the hide. It's important that the lacing not be done tightly at this stage, so the hide will still be laying on the ground. Then go to the tail end and repeat (#3 and #4), also working towards the sides of the hide. Once more, the hide should still be laying flat on the ground after these two bundles are added to the hide. Then go to the middle of each side, and lace up the rest of the hide, #5 and #6 going towards the head, #7 and #8 going towards the tail. This ordering of the lacing ropes is very important,

as the hide can otherwise be strung lopsided, twisted, or off center so it can't be stretched taut, rendering it virtually impossible to scrape evenly. So take your time with the lacing. Eventually you'll get the hang of it and praise my instructions.

After making sure the hide is still centered on the frame, return to the same ordering and continue gradually tightening down the hide. After tightening each rope, the loose ends can be wrapped around the frame and secured with a half hitch and bow knot, or tied to one of the lacing holes (*above right*). I do it both ways, and it just depends on what length of rope is left over. Depending on the size of the hide you're framing, it may be that with some hides, you won't need any of the bundles used on the sides (#5 thru #8); or, you may need to add in one or more bundles. Eventually, if you keep up the order, the hide will draw as tight as it can go and be centered (like the deerskin I've framed *above left* and the skin the Indian woman is working back in the first chapter). Very good, because that's where you want matters to be at this point. It sounds like a lot, but once you've got the hang of it, you can frame a hide in 10 to 15 minutes. And the good news is that you won't be lacing this hide up on this frame again. Just this one time. When it does finally come off, you will finish it immediately into beautiful white buckskin. Let's keep going, we've a bit more work to do.

Raise and secure the frame

The time has come to raise the frame and place it against a wall (most any wall will do), two upright posts set in the ground, or even a sturdy tree as I've done in many of the photos here. Use whatever is available or you can put together. But bear in mind that wherever you set the frame, a whole lot of "flesh scrapings" are going to hit the ground underneath. However you do it, the frame needs to be brought up vertically at a slight angle to keep it from falling over on you. Set the frame so that the neck of the hide is pointing up. Larger frames carrying larger hides may have to be set sideways, otherwise, you will have to build a scaffold as I did with the full bison hide during my horse trek.

Once up, you'll now notice that the hide is probably sagging somewhat on the frame. This is normal. Once again, lace it up following the same ordering as before, and the hide will stay centered and taut. Once this is done, it's time to start working the hide. But bear in mind, at any time the hide begins to sag, stop your work and lace it up taut. Typically this happens 3 or more times during the flesh scraping process, which is about to happen.

De-flesh the hide

Unless the hunter is an expert butcher, the flesh side of the hide typically has clumps of clinging residual meat, fat, and various strands of subcutaneous fiber, all attached to the underlying tissue comprising the main body of the skin, called the "dermis" or "true skin." Our immediate objective is to remove all of this "trash," leaving just the dermis. On the other side of the skin (what was the hair side) is the outer skin or "grain" of the dermis, also called the "epidermis." We'll remove that layer later. Right now, our focus is to clear debris from the flesh side of the dermis.

Here's where the scraper comes into action. I use it and also my fingers (occasionally) to scrape and peel things off the dermis. You'll just need to experiment and feel the situation out to get the hang of it. Once you do, you'll know how much pressure is needed to bear down on the hide with that scraper, and

(*Left*) I use long forceful strokes with the scraper, and as seen from the backside you can really appreciate the great elasticity of the deer skin. (*Right*) Long strands and bands of adhering tissue can be pulled loose from the dermis with your fingers.

when to pull things loose and remove with your hands, but not your teeth. Once you're an expert like me, you'll get it all done in 5 to 10 minutes, depending on the size of the hide and how much the hunter left you to deal with. You'll probably need to add tension to the ropes along the way as the hide will tend to stretch as stuff is removed. Natural tanners actually enjoy this step, because you feel like you've finally done something to the hide yourself, instead of the salt, lime, and delimer doing all the work. We also like making physical contact with the hide with our hands and tools — it's what natural tanning is all about. Hopefully, some of my photos will help you figure it out too. You're going to do great! You're learning, so have patience and give yourself some leeway for making mistakes. You can throw the "scrapings" on the ground into the garbage or into the woods or back forty — because it'll all be gone before sunrise.

When you're done, or think you're done, let the skin dry in the sun. You want it to completely dry out into rawhide. This is why I tan during the summer. Hot summers speed up the process. For this reason, you might also want to do the scraping in the shade in the early morning hours to spare yourself some heat stroke, then set the framed hide in the direct sun to dry during the hottest time of the day. If it happens to rain on your hide, no problem. Just let it dry out the next day. Now, if it's going to be raining for a spell, I would put the frame in an enclosed shed and let it dry out in there. Then when the rain stops, bring it back out into the sun to finish drying it out.

Remove the grain (epidermis)

When the skin is completely dried out, we're ready to remove the grain (epidermis). The grain has to be removed or it will stiffen the finished buckskin. We don't want that. We want beautiful, soft white buckskin suede — the prized result!

File or grind your scraper blade until it's super sharp. Drag it down the center of the hide, starting at the neck (at the top of the frame). As you did with defleshing, bear down just enough to shave the grain off. This will take practice to learn and confirm. Continue to shave the entire hide, but stay away from the ropes so you don't cut them. You can shave in all directions, the objective being to

Graining the hide is easy, but the scraper blade needs to be very sharp to be effective. To remove all the epidermis, rotate the frame 90 degrees as I've down here so that its being scraped in two directions.

remove all the grain. You don't need to thin the hide down anymore than what removes the grain layer. Some thicker hides may possess a thicker layer of grain, so it may take a bit more work to get it off. Some fanatics and perfectionists will finish the skin by smoothing it with heavy sandpaper after they do the scraping. I don't, and you don't need to do it either. You can make beautiful buckskin without any sanding.

Soak the hide in water

Once you're done graining, or you think it's done, we have to soak the hide on the frame. I sense you're thinking another trip to the hardware store is coming. Possibly, but it will depend. If you have a pond or stream on your property, you can lower the frame into it as I've done with most of my tanning (*above*). Otherwise you'll have to build a small makeshift pool, or find a commercial one big enough to fit the frame. It doesn't need to be more than a foot deep. I've made one with boards that looks like a sand box. Line it with Visqueen and then fill it with water. Place the frame with hide so that the staples are facing down; the weight of the frame will then keep the hide submerged. Leave it in the water overnight.

Prepare your pre-tanning ingredients

These are ingredients that we are going to add to the skin and let them soak in. Here's what I use to produce a naturally occurring white color to the buckskin when it's done (but not yet tanned). For an average deer skin, pick up 2 to 3 pounds of pork brains from the grocery store. That's right, some people eat the stuff, but don't ask me why or how. Also get a gallon container of *pure* neat's-foot oil, but avoid the neat's-foot oil compound, which is a blend of the pure stuff, plus other animals oils and petroleum products. This oil is made from cooked and rendered cattle legs and feet (not the hooves). You may have to order this online to find this pure version. You can use other animal organs such as liver, but they will tend to darken the buckskin. That won't be an issue if you intend to smoke tan the white buckskin later. For your first time around, leave the liver out and use the brains and neat's-foot oil.

In a cooking pot you will use for future tanning (*right, above*), add the brains and a quart of water and simmer until the brains are cooked through — just a few minutes. Adding water makes them easier to mash, apply and spread further. What I do next is optional but recommended: get a cheap blender from Walmart and reduce the brains to a pulp. If too thick to pour, add a little warm water. Then pour the whole mash into a bucket or plastic milk jug (*right, below*). Then add half a cup of the neat's-foot oil and mix it in.

What these ingredients do is lubricate the fibers. The brains, I find, also give "body" or fullness to the finished skin. The oil super lubricates the fibers. So, the two

Those are pork brains I'm cooking in the pot. This photo was taken over 40 years ago, and somehow I've kept it all these years.

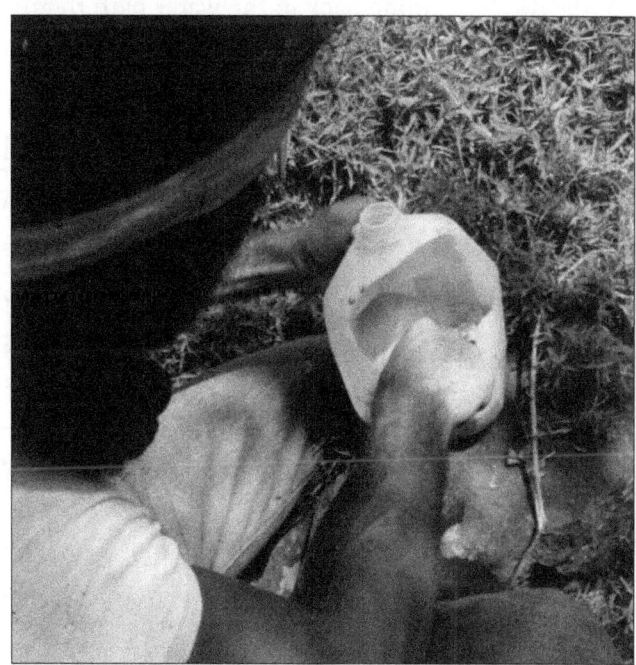

I've carved out a section of a plastic milk carton to hold the brain mash. With the carton handle to one side, it's easier to hold and use than a bucket.

work well together. I have done this with just the brains, but experience has taught me that I get, if not a superior white buckskin, then buckskin that is easier to finish when I use brains and oil together. You'll come to your own conclusion in time.

Add pre-tanning ingredients to skin

Remove the frame and hide from the water bath and secure it upright as before. Using your scraper, squeegee as much water from the dermis as you can. Do this to both sides of the hide. Continue until the surface of the hide is slightly damp, but definitely not dried out anywhere while still on the frame. Because it will end up as rawhide. We don't want that!

Next, add your pre-tanning mixture to the skin. I use a broad paint brush (*facing page*). Put a thick coat on both sides right out to the edges of the skin. Let it soak in all day in the hot sun. If there is left over mash, refrigerate it because we're going to use more, a lot more, before we're done.

Add more pre-tanning ingredients

My rule of thumb is to add the brain mash three times. But I soak and squeegee the skin each time before adding fresh ingredients. This means putting the frame back in the water bath the night before each time. The skin has to be rehydrated first. Scraping the skin stretches the dermal fibers, enabling the dermis to absorb more lubricating ingredients each time. This is really important when it comes to tanning skins that are really thick, like elk and moose. So, as before, scrape both sides of the skin — and you'll probably notice the skin is really stretching due to the lubrication. That's good. Let the excess brains fall to the ground. Now, bring out your new batch of warm mash and brush it on both sides. Once more, let the mash soak in and the skin dry thoroughly while in the hot sun. Don't worry, the skin won't rot if you keep it in the sun and let it dry out completely. What you're making is "leather jerky," in fact, Indians used their tanning racks for jerking meat.

By the third braining, if not the second, you'll notice that the dried hide has become opaque rather than somewhat translucent — like before you added the ingredients the first time. In fact, this is important. Areas still translucent (i.e., not opaque) tend not to finish into buckskin but remain hard — rawhide, in other words. Only on the rarest occasions have I had to "re-brain" the skins more than

three times to get the mash thoroughly "stuffed" into the dermis. But if that's what it takes, do it.

So that you know, when I was tanning 15 to 20 skins at a time for Larry and others years ago, I used multiple tanning frames. They were all over the place. As soon as the skins were opaque, I removed them from the frames and new skins were laced on. In this way, I could keep the hides moving forward at various stages at the same time. You really want to know what your doing when you're doing that many all at once! But I didn't do anything different for any of those hides than what I'm explaining here.

We're getting close to the finishing step. We're going to have beautiful, soft, white buckskin in our hands. But there's one more thing we need to do first.

Remove hide from frame

After scraping the hide of excess ingredients for the last time, you will notice one of nature's miracles: what was rawhide, has now become more like leather (technically, "un-tanned leather," which I will explain shortly), than raw skin. And, if you've followed my directions diligently, it will be very white or slightly off-white. Blood stains that the hunter may have introduced into the dermis during skinning

may be apparent in some spots, but hopefully not!

Bringing the hide to finish can be tricky when first learning. As the scraping commences (on both sides), the scraper will begin to meet with too much drag to slide freely across the skin. This is a critical point in the process. The hide must be cut loose from the frame at the first sign of drag resistance, otherwise, the dermis will "threaten" to dry out on you and become rawhide. Not good! So, once more, what you do is cut the hide loose from the frame while the dermis is still slightly damp. Very important! Cut just inside the slots in the skin so as not to cut the lacing ropes (*left*). Continue all the way around the hide (*facing page*), until it's

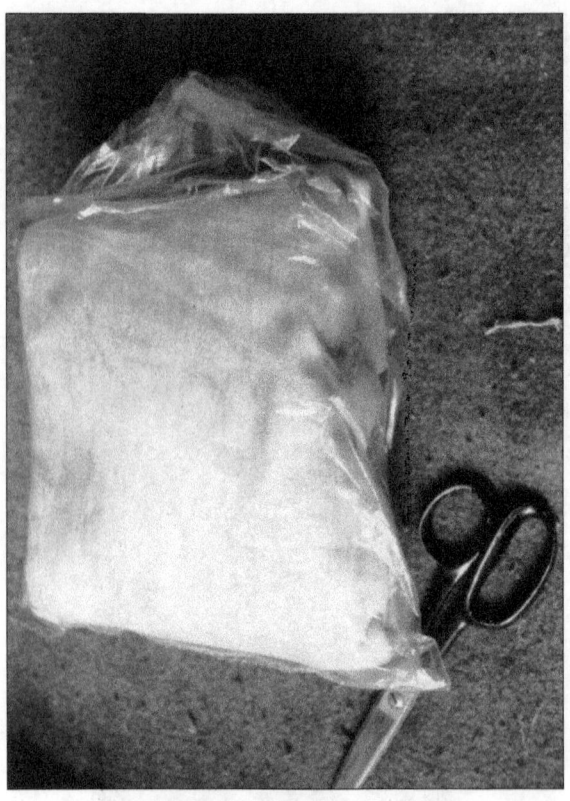
Bag your hide and take a well-earned break!

cut loose. You'll want a sharp edge on your hunter's knife to make these cuts.

Now you have a choice to make with what you want to do next. If you want to put the hide aside, take a break, and deal with it the next day or several hours later, fold it up neatly and put it in a large zip lock bag or other air tight container (*left*). Put it in the refrigerator. When doing large numbers of hides, I will put the bagged hides in the freezer, which will keep them from rotting for a year or more. Your other choice is to keep working the hide, although you can stop at any time and put the hide under refrigeration if you need a break. Assuming the work is still on, let's continue.

What you do now is lay the skin between two large towels and roll all three up together. I'll twist the bundle to ring out whatever moisture I can. I usually keep several sets of towels on hand during the finishing so they can absorb any large amounts of excess moisture at the hide's surface while I take a short break (a few minutes only at a time). The time has come to finish the skin and convert it into beautiful white suede.

Rub the skin into buckskin

To finish the skin and turn it into buckskin, we will rub the hide over a $3/8$ in. thick braided polyethylene rope tied between two eye bolts or other forms of attachment to secure the ends of the rope. On this note, let's go back to that ring of hide still hanging on your tanning frame (*facing page*).

You can make rope from three of those rings, that is, once you've done enough hides! Remove your rope bundles then coil and tie them off individually. Drop them into a bucket of warm soapy water so they can come clean. Dry them out for future use. Take the ring and wash it off also in a bucket of warm soapy water. What I did at my cabin in the mountains where all these photos were taken, was set two t-posts about 10–12 feet apart. I then cut the ring once to make

You can make "semi-tanned" rawhide rope from the ring of skin on the tanning frame. Just leave enough skin around the slits when you're cutting the hide off. Notice the other tanning frames in the background; one is loaded and ready for the hide's final soaking. Bag and freeze multiple pre-tanned hides for rubbing later.

a long strand. I opened up one of the slits and looped it around the t-post. At the other end, I put a short length of a branch through another slit. Next, I began twisting the entire length until it would twist no more. I then removed the branch and put a length of rope in the slit and tied it to the other t-post. Finally, I trimmed off any protruding flaps of skin along the length of the "rope" and let it dry in the sun. A thin rawhide rope was the result. You can take three of these

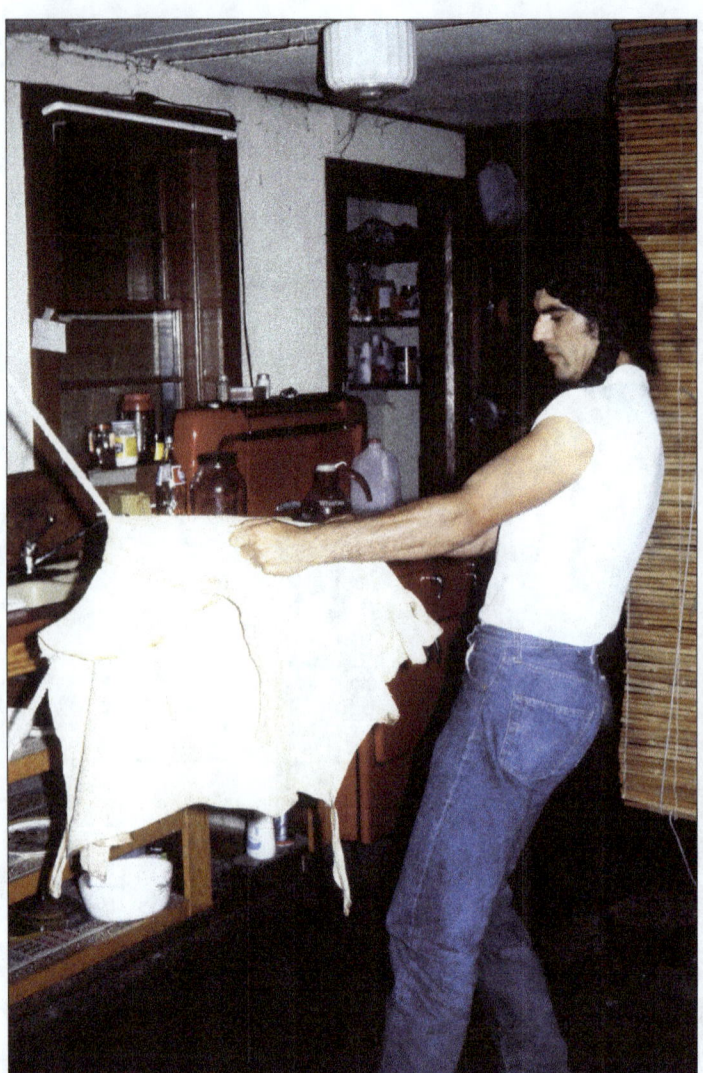 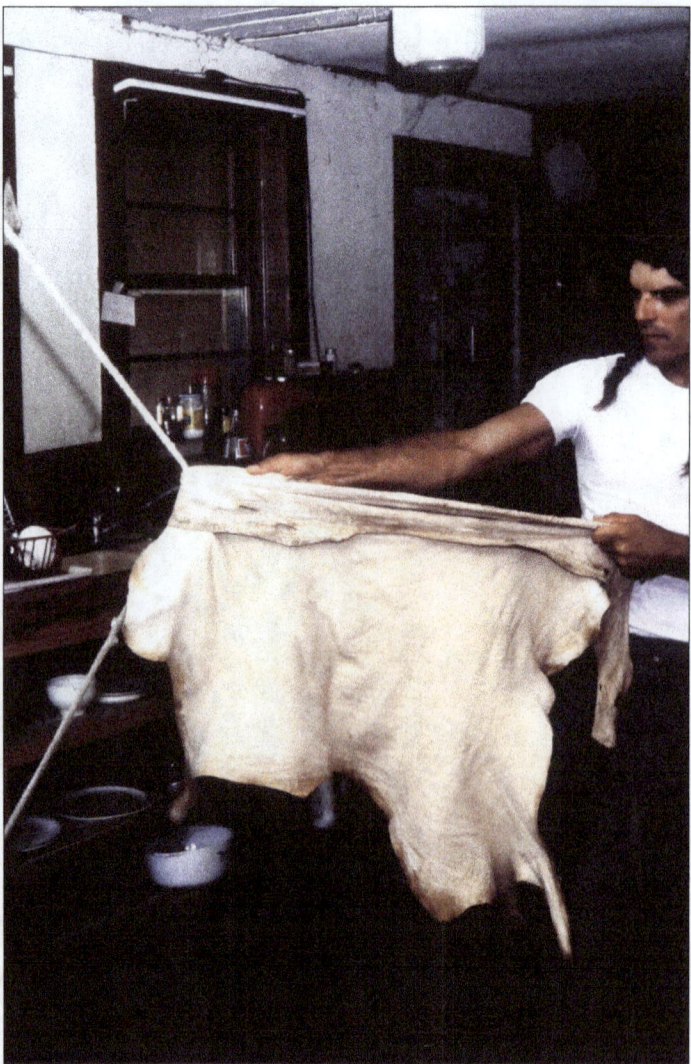

ropes, soak them until soft and braid them together between the t-posts. Use a 3-strand braiding method and they'll stay together. It's a bit of work, but the result works well for rubbing hides to finish.

Rubbing is stand-up work and we're going to really lay into the skin with our weight as we pull it back and forth across the rope (*above, left*). There's an effective way to do this: with clean bare hands, start at the neck and work half way down the hide, stop reverse it and begin at the tail working down towards the middle. Then flip the hide side ways and work towards the middle (*above, right*), then turn it around and work towards the middle from the other side. Flip the hide over and do the same thing to the other side. This way the entire hide is stretched uniformly. If you have a pulling partner, have him or her do the opposite side. Rotating gives you both a break.

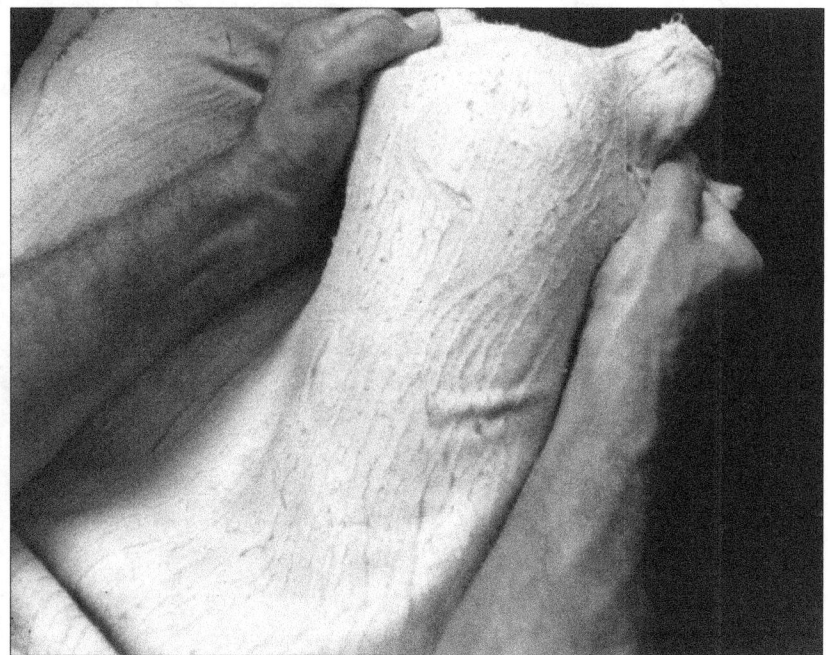

When both sides have been stretched across the rope, put it back between two new dry towels. Let it "rest" there for a few minutes while absorbing moisture that's wicked to the surface. Come to think of it, there are several ways to do this, but I had long forgotten until I opened the box containing my tanning manuscript papers from 40 years ago (*above, left*). As you can see, I put the bundle of towels and hide onto the stretching rope and gave it a pretty vigorous twist to lock it all in. That's one way to step up the wicking effect!

While between the towels, the dermis will begin to gather into its natural "tanned" thickness. This is to be expected and is good — but only tentative if you're going to take your break. Areas of minimal moisture within the dermis can still revert to rawhide if not wicked out by rubbing. So, either the hide is in the towels for a brief stay, or it goes into the refrigerator — or we keep going. Let's keep going.

As before, continue rubbing the skin across the rope, following the same protocol. It's really important to stretch the hide as it dries. You can also lay it over your knee and pull on it (*above, right*). This serves two objectives: to maintain the flexibility of the fibers

The finished buckskin is bright white, almost blindingly so in the direct sun. Hard to see, but I'm sharpening my hunter's knife for one last step: we need to stretch the rumpled hide so that it lies flat.

constituting the dermis, and to draw unwanted moisture to the surface of the skin where ambient heat (and your pants!) can do their work to desiccate the dermis. As the moisture finally gives way completely, or almost completely, the skin will become buckskin in your hands (*facing page*). The brain mash supplants (replaces) the water, coating the entire fibrous body of the dermis. Excess mash, if any, is absorbed by the towels.

You'll probably be excited by the buckskin. But you're still not done. All the tugging and pulling naturally causes the dermis to rumple and not lay flat. This brings us to the last step of the pre-tanning phase.

Stretch the buckskin in the finishing frame

The whole purpose here is to stretch the buckskin so that it will lay flat on a level surface. As such, it will be more useful for making things or just showing your work off. We'll use what I call the "finishing frame." This is a somewhat smaller version of the fleshing frame just used. The proportions are the same, again just smaller. I had different fleshing/graining and finishing frames to fit different size hides: deer, elk/moose, and bison.

You'll want to keep your finishing frame "clean," and I think you've got the picture if you want a finished buckskin that isn't soiled. Lay your buckskin down on a clean surface and make it lay as flat as you can. Make the frame about six inches longer and wider than the buckskin. Compare those dimensions with the fleshing frame. Put the frame together just like the fleshing one, with 2 x 4s, corner braces, and fencing staples. I recommend using new lacing ropes.

Just like you did with the raw skin, cut slits all around the buckskin. Using clean ropes, lace it up just like you did it on the fleshing frame. Tighten it down. Brace the frame it against a wall or other support and knead the entire buckskin with the heel of your hand. Put some effort into the kneading because your objective is to stretch the buckskin. Knead on both sides. As you do, the buckskin will begin to sag — tighten up the ropes. Leave it over night, and come check it in the morning. If it's sagging at all knead it some more. Chances are it remained taught over night. If that's the case, the buckskin is finished. Well, maybe not. Read on.

Tan the buckskin

Now I need to explain the difference between "pre-tanned" and "tanned" buckskin, because it will help you to decide what you want to do next with your white buckskin. First, I need to expand on the definition of tanning I gave up front in the first chapter. Technically, tanning means altering the protein (collagen) structure of the skin (dermis, in the case of suede buckskin) to prevent its return to the "rawhide" state and also to prevent decomposition. Over a century ago, industrial tanning operations used the bark of oak trees, which were rich in the chemical tannin. The term tannin is derived from the Latin word *tannāre* (meaning "oak bark"), from which the common term "tanning" comes from. As the Industrial Revolution progressed, other chemical-based ingredients were deployed besides tannin. Many of these are hazardous substances and the tanning industry eventually developed a well-earned reputation as "polluters" of the environment. That's another issue I won't go into in this book, except to say natural tanning doesn't pollute.

Brains and neat's-foot oil don't actually tan the hide, because they don't alter the dermis molecularly. They only lubricate the fibers constituting the dermis. Consequently, if your white (or crème-colored) buckskin gets wet, and you don't return it to the rubbing rope, it will revert to rawhide, or at best the stiff opaque finish we faced earlier. As long as you keep it from getting wet, it truly is a beautiful piece of "ersatz" leather to display or make things with. In writing this book, I have assumed that you might want it tanned so that the dermal structure meets the technical definition of tanning. And so you don't have to worry about it getting wet. You're not alone. Indians didn't either! What they did was smoke their buckskins with a smudge fire. The warm smoke contains the naturally occurring compound *aldehyde* which, like tannin, does chemically alter the structure of the dermis.[1] The effect is to sustain the buckskin in pretty much the same state before it was smoked. However, the smoke naturally darkens the hide, which, as it turns out, many reenactment buffs want. But it can be washed in warm soapy water to restore much of its pre-smoked appearance, in fact, giving it what I think of as the true "buckskin color" (*facing page*) This makes sense because smoked buckskin is traditionally washed like you would any garment that needs cleaning.

There are different ways to "smoke tan" your buckskin, including lacing it into a bag and hanging it over a smudge fire (no different than adding wood chips to your barbeque to smoke your food). The risk is that the hot coals can burn the hide; added wood chips can do the same. You don't want that to happen! Here's

---

[1] I actually wrote a paper about the chemical reaction involved with smoke tanning back in the late 1970s, which was reviewed and critiqued by Jean J. Tancous, a scientist (now retired) at the Tanners Council Laboratory, housed at the University of Cincinnati. I've appended that paper at the back of this book, including Jean's comments

(*Top*) I smoke tanned this deer skin so many years ago I can't remember when exactly. For years I laid it over a banister in my home for visitors to touch and slide their hands over. Eventually, it left a dark, soiled band down the center of the back. On either side, though, you can see the rich honey color imparted by the smoke. (*Below*) After decades, I decided recently to throw it in the washing machine with Tide and 20 Mule Team Borax, because it really needed it. The band has faded, and so has the smoke tan effect. Repeated washings will continue to lighten the hide. You can dry it in a dryer machine, but use a low heat setting.

19th century Sioux war shirt with pony beads, porcupine quills, smoked-tanned buckskin, maidenhair fern stem, human hair, horsehair, dye, and feather.

what I recommend instead, especially if you're going to be doing more buckskins in the future. Get a large box, like one of those they ship refrigerators in. Inquire at your local appliance store, I'm sure they wouldn't mind giving you one. Make a little clothesline or closet rod near the top of the box, and hang your hide from it using strings passed through the slots at the neck and shoulders of the buckskin. Now you can put a pan of briquettes with moist wood chips at the bottom of the box (which you've cut out), on a layer of bricks, well below the hanging buckskin. You want to create a dense, warm smoke inside the box. I have done this, cutting a door on one side of the box (use a box cutter) to get in and out to feed the wood chips and check on the buckskin. On one occasion, a friend and I used his wood smoker, running a horizontal vent pipe into the box! That really worked well. You can experiment with other ideas. Be creative, and be practical!

Smoke the hide all day long. The smudge should keep the buckskin warm during the smoking, but not so hot as to deteriorate (as in melt) the fibers. You can smoke it over several days if you want. When the dermis is thoroughly penetrated (the dermis will have changed color), remove the buckskin from the box.

Fold and put it in a plastic zip-loc bag to "cure" for a day or two (or as long as you want).

You're done! What you do with buckskin next is entirely up to you. Be sure to show it off to others! Now, let's move on to bison tanning.

Bison Buckskin

Like many contemporary buckskinners, I became intrigued with how Indians tanned bison (buffalo) hides. And for that matter, how they would have tanned the white man's cowhides, because — as I learned early on — they did. The hides used in the tipis at Disneyland were commercially tanned, not by the Indians Disney brought there. My interest in Indian tanning, which I now think of and call "natural tanning," remained dormant within me 20 years after the Disney experience. It was rekindled immediately after I got out of the Army in January of 1970.

I had just returned from overseas and became one of those vets who opposed the Vietnam war, a debacle that was likely the greatest military blunder in the history of our country. Disillusioned by our government's intrusion into the lives of the Vietnamese people, I began to run with the then burgeoning population of "counterculture" dropouts. It was a great time, meeting all sorts of interesting people who shared a common thread in life — "things need to change." I'd like to digress into all of that, but friends and colleagues want me to make that whole period, and what happened afterwards, a book of its own. By the end of 1970, I stumbled upon a huge commune on the coast of Mendocino in California. There were hundreds of "outcasts," free-thinkers, draft dodgers, philosophers, anarchists, remnants of the hippy days, a few real Indians, and daily visits from curious neighbors and even magazines who wanted a story. It was crazy, and I didn't stay long. But long enough to meet this woman who was living in a canvas tipi she had bought somewhere. It was a flashback to the early 1950s. My interest in American Indian culture, including their tanning methods, was resurrected.

There was no Internet back then, or computers, or cell phones, just snail mail, typewriters, and old time telephones that you dialed with your finger. From Union Hide in Oakland, California, I got raw deer and calf skins to experiment on. I discovered old manuscripts about Indian tanning at the University of California in Berkeley. That's when I first became aware that animal organs were used to tan. Brains were at the top of the list in virtually every historical account. About this time, 1973, I crossed paths with Larry Belitz's book, *Brain Tanning the Sioux Way*. I tried his method, although it required several letters and phone calls to get better clarification. Always helpful, he also sent me a sharpened metal blade for a scraper. I then got real good at tanning deer buckskin. Good enough that he paid me to tan for him! I've lost track of how many I tanned for him.

The cow skins I got from Union Hide didn't respond to the brain tanning. Larry wasn't as clear about this, and I put it aside for several more years. Then, during the winter of 1983, after much investigation and experimentation, I solved the bison tanning mystery (as I saw it). It was probably the most profound learning journey into natural tanning of my life. It's a story full of twists and turns, including four enlightening trips to the Western History Collection of the University of Oklahoma, the Tanner's Council Laboratory (University of Cincinnati), the Chicago Field Museum, and a return to Union Hide, including it's huge cow and bison tanning operation in California's San Joaquin Valley. It's a story I need to tell here, because it's all about what happened and didn't happen in the old Indian tanning camps. There's a whole lot of misinformation, some of it pure myth or dishonesty, floating around out there among brain tan aficionados, and I think what I learned should help clear some of this up. And actually help tanners, old and new stumped by bison hide tanning.

But first, let me put matters in the timeline of events that led to the discovery.

Tanners Council Laboratory, University of Cincinnati

During the late 1970s, I began to turn my attentions back to the problem of bison hide tanning. A logical place to start among other possibilities was to see what scientists of the commercial tanning industry might know. With a little research I found the Tanners Council Laboratory, located on the campus of the University of Cincinnati. It served both as a research and teaching arm of the university, focusing on tanning science. It was paid for by the tanning industry itself.

One of the scientists there was a wonderfully helpful lady by the name of Jean J. Tancous. She invited me to come use the Council's library and to seek answers to my questions about brain tan bison tanning. She and the library turned out to be a real godsend because the experience enabled me to elucidate the facts of the matter about what brains can and cannot do. Not surprisingly, the industry is well aware of "primitive tanning" because its very roots go back to that. I set to work reading everything I could about tanning, including what primitive tanning is at its molecular level. I asked Jean if she would read and critique a paper I planned to write about my findings. She agreed and I've appended it at the back of this book with other source material. Bear in mind, the science and scientific language of tanning has progressed since then, and with it has come new insights into the biochemical interactions between tanning agents and animal skins. But the science I learned at the Tanner's Council laboratory, notwithstanding the above, still applies today relative to bison tanning "the natural way."

First, I studied the architecture of the dermal fibers themselves. Bison and cattle are both members of the genera bovine (Bovinae, a sub-family of Bovidae), ungulates with cloven hooves. The fibers of their hides reticulate (cross each other like a net), and are, thus, less flexible than hides of the deer family, whose fibers are more striated and prone to stretching. Anyone whose "brain tanned" deer and attempted bison hides knows what I'm talking about. So, it was clear from the industry's science, reticulated fibers simply stand in the way of brain tanning.

But what I also found out is that the brains lacked the chemical agents to alter the fibrous proteins (collagens) constituting the dermis of bison or deer. No surprise, by now I already knew that from experience. But what I didn't know is that there are a class of *naturally occurring* and highly reactive organic compounds that can and do alter the proteins of the dermis of any animal skin. These are called *aldehydes* and I describe how they work in my appended bison tanning paper. I learned also that they occur naturally in smoke, which explained their effect on the buckskin. But they also arise in marine oils that can be rendered from fish by boiling, unlike in brains and neat's-foot oil that can't tan anything — unless smoke or fish oil are introduced. Fish oil, when heated, oxidizes (a complex chemical change) and produces aldehydes like those produced in warm smoke. Add fish oil to the brain/liver/fat mash, I speculated, and you have a mixture that "fills," lubricates and tans the dermis and it's complex maze of proteins. All of this now made sense to me. I could experiment with all these ingredients. At this time I was living in a cabin with 40 acres in the Boston Mountains of North Arkansas with my horses. I headed back home and finished my paper. Jean later wrote me to say, "I wish my grad students would write a thesis this good!"

Western History Collection, University of Oklahoma

About this time, 1980-81 as I recall, I received a photo of a white hide tipi with a horse tied to a pole out front. The owner of the tipi said it was made of bison hides and they had brain tanned them the Indian way. A sample swatch sent to me indicated that the beautiful white leather was soft as deer and very supple.

"How could this be," I asked myself. I wrote back about the tanning but the response was strangely evasive and not at all specific beyond the usual brain tan claims and rehetoric. I was pretty convinced that I knew better now, so I decided not to be confrontational and put the matter aside. But fate would have it otherwise. A friend visiting me at the time needed a ride from Arkansas back to their home in Colorado. I agreed to take them there, and on the way, and only by chance, did we run into a large tannery in, as I recall (but may have it wrong), Colorado Springs. We stopped in to check it out. It may have been after hours because the owner, an older German man I think judging by his accent, was there alone. I expressed interest in what he did and he offered a short tour. We were passing through his office when I noticed a photograph in a frame on his desk. It was the same photograph of the tipi with the horse. I asked him where he got it. I was shocked to hear him say that he tanned the hides in his factory for the person who then (ostensibly) put it together. I asked him if they were "brain tanned." He laughed and said, "No." Until now, I haven't mentioned this encounter with anyone.

My intuition was that my current investigative path would lead me to the truth of the matter concerning any such claims. Oddly, about the same time I heard about, and contacted, another purported bison brain tanner. Again, a sample swatch of the leather sent to me struck me as being, well, fraudulent. I did manage to get a phone number and a house mate answered. They told me the tanner actually slept in their bed covered with buffalo hides finished and unfinished. I dropped that lead like a hot potato. If that was the way it had to be done, sleeping with raw skins, I was done with bison tanning altogether. Kajeeezzzz. I pushed on.

On my agenda during these early years of investigation was to visit the prestigious Western History Collections at the University of Oklahoma in Norman. I could get there in a hard day's drive from my cabin. I'd heard a bit about its manuscripts dealing with 19th century Native American culture. The librarian there was as friendly and helpful with my pursuit as Jean back at the Tanners Laboratory. I decided to stay a week and dig into their archives to see what I could come up with related to Indian tanning. There was a lot, but a lot of the same old baloney. Mainly observers commenting about a process they clearly didn't understand and didn't do themselves. By now, you should get the picture from producing your own deer buckskin. You really have to do it, to truly understand it.

By the end of the week, I was ready to give up when the librarian passed me an old 1904 newspaper clipping about Southern Cheyenne Indians living in Oklahoma making a hide tipi at the direction of the American ethnographer, James Mooney (1861-1921). This was before Oklahoma's statehood in 1907. Before then it was called the Oklahoma Territory, and before that Indian Territory, following the U.S. Government's forced relocation of Indians mainly from the Southeastern U.S. and the southernmost Great Plains. Not a good time for Indians, to say the least.

Mooney, so I came to learn, had great respect for Indians and wanted the world to know the truth about their cultures from their own mouths and for posterity. He wanted to display the tipi at the St. Louis (Missouri) World Exposition in 1904, after which, it would be given to the Field Columbian Museum (as it was called then) in Chicago. Tribal members agreed to the project. Tanning and construction of the tipi began in early spring of 1903. I pondered, did Mooney keep notes specifically about that project? Moreover, could the tipi still be at the Chicago museum nearly 75 years later? I returned home to figure out what I would do next.

Logically, driving north to the Field Museum to see the tipi was at the top of my list. I called the museum to make an appointment. The tipi, they told me, was still there. I got one of the department bureaucrats on the phone only to be told that I couldn't see it because it was locked in a special climate controlled area of the museum where the public wasn't allowed. My protests did no good. I learned later that it had been brought out once or twice in the past for viewing, but no such plans were in the making in the present. Nor did they possess or know anything about Mooney's notes, if they even existed. Sensing my despair, they suggested that I contact a priest, Father Peter Powell, who was a Research Associate at the Newberry Library in Chicago, which housed, I was told, an extensive library on Native American culture. Powell, they suggested, might know something. I did, but Powell knew nothing and suggested that I contact the Smithsonian Institution, where the Bureau of American Ethnology (BAE) had collections and documents also treating Native American history. "Why hadn't I thought of that?" I asked myself, recalling from the news article that the BAE was Mooney's employer back then.

I had never been to the Smithsonian, and Powell made reference to its own

Chicago's Field Museum, basement home to the Cheyenne tipi for 112 years.

collections of Native American artifacts. I was ready to make plans to go when fate would intervene and send me in another direction. The BAE would have to wait.

Union Hide - Oakland, California

Through intermediaries I had accepted an invitation to teach "Indian tanning" to naturalists working for the Coyote Hills Regional Park, part of the East Bay Regional Parks system in central California. This was in the early 1980s, and they wanted me to come now. I agreed, and planned to stay one month, as my horseshoeing business in the Ozarks had really expanded, and clients were concerned I might never return. It was a concern that eventually came true. In the meanwhile, my horses stayed at my cabin, and a housemate was found to watch over them. I was given residence at one of the park's ranger barracks bordering on the San Francisco Bay, not far north of San Jose. This put me back in the vicinity of Union Hide — and a source of bison hides. Things seemed to be lining up.

The vice-president of Union Hide, and shortly in 1983 its new president, Joe Katzburg, had helped me out a decade earlier with those calf hides. I made contact with him again as soon as I arrived in the Bay Area. He was interested in my tanning project, and graciously flew me in his plane to the company's massive tanning operation in central California, which served the cattle industry. Union Hide was also the largest bison meat processor and commercial tanner of bison hides on the west coast, if not the entire U.S. I asked Joe if it were possible to get a bison hide with the hair removed and thinned somehow. I had read various accounts, historical and contemporary, that stated the bison hide must be thinned down if it is to soften and tan with brains. I would test this claim. Not only de-haired, Joe promised, they could thin it down as much as I wanted, and which they did with this incredible "slicing" machine I had never seen before. It had a razor sharp, long-bladed knife, four or five feet wide positioned against an equally long, rotating metal roller that could be set as close to the blade as they wanted. An untanned hide came down a conveyer belt, which was then drawn against the blade by the roller — sort of like squeezing clothes through one of those old time ringer washing machines — thinning the hide down to any thickness. It was amazing to see. I asked the technician if he could first split the hide in two down the middle, which would make for easier handling. He could, and handed me half a raw bison skin with the epidermis (grain) removed, and a third of the dermis removed too. It was very thin, to say the least. I also got a de-haired calf skin.

I brought these two hides to the park where I was staying, and set to work on them. Surely, I reasoned, if all it took was a thin hide to brain tan the bison (or the naturally thin calf hide — and remember, bison and domestic bovine collagen structure is basically the same), this had to work. It didn't. No matter how many coatings of brain mash I stuffed into the dermis, no matter how many scrapings and kneading, no matter how much I tugged and pulled over the rope, the skin stiffened up. Not exactly into rawhide, but a very close cousin! I couldn't begin to imagine accomplishing a thing with a bison bull hide! Conceivably, if the bison half I worked on were roughed-up enough, it could be draped over a set of tipi poles, but not much more. And so thinned down, I couldn't see it enduring much of a beating from storms and handling and remain in one piece. I concluded, and accurately so, brain mash can't tan. I returned home to my cabin after successfully teaching deer buckskin to the park naturalists.

Chicago Field Museum

You have to understand that amid all of this, I was busy as heck on several fronts as a full time farrier (horseshoer) in Arkansas and, beginning in 1982, a regular visitor to the U.S. Great Basin, where I had initiated a four year study of the hooves and lifestyles of America's wild, free-roaming horses (aka, "mustangs"). I decided to rent a room from one of the park rangers in the Bay Area, where I had developed a small shoeing clientele during my weekends off at the park, then fly back to Arkansas to train a lady to take over my hoof care business, and visit wild horses in between. This went on for most of 1982 and early 1983, when I ended my horseshoeing business in Arkansas (I had by then created a new one in California).

In the middle of all of this, I eventually called the Smithsonian and got museum curator John Ewers (famous in his own right as an ethnologist) who directed me to James Glenn, an archivist for the National Anthropological Archives. To my delight, Mooney's notes were there. Sparing me a long trip to Washington (I was now in California), he could send them to me. On April 18th, 1983, I received six pages of Mooney's notes from Glenn, describing in great detail (enough for me anyway as an experienced brain tanner) the tanning of 27 hides that went into the Cheyenne tipi. The notes revealed that a dozen or so Southern Cheyenne woman did the work. The BAE catalogue file reads verbatim:

> Mooney, James. Miscellaneous notes on the Cheyenne. 1903-1906.
> Approx. 75 pp.
> Difficult script, but legible to reader familiar with Mooney's writing and abbreviations. Includes day-by-day account of hide-dressing process, Apl. 28-May 28, 1903. Corresponding snapshots by Mooney (somewhat blurred) are in BAE photographic files, 'original prints' series.

While the photos were "somewhat blurred," they were clear enough for me to understand what these women were doing. For sure, it was my good fortune that Mooney kept prodigious and detailed notes and that I was able to get copies from the Smithsonian. It was my misfortune, however, that Mooney's hand writing was deplorable, even worse than medical doctors, if you can imagine that. In fact, his hand writing was so illegible that it was an issue for Mooney at the Bureau of Ethnology in Washington, D.C., whose bureaucrats agreed to funding his project with considerable consternation, at one point warning him to spend time transcribing his notes into legibility — or else. As I scanned the six pages, I realized I couldn't read a word of it. To say the least, "deplorable" is being kind and I am fully in accord and sympathetic with the BAE overseers a century later!

I decided to return once more to the University of Oklahoma several months later to talk with Dr. John Moore in the Anthropology department. Moore told me he had Mooney's notes and that they were transcribed. Elated, I flew to the university in November of 1983 to see his transcriptions. I should have stayed home. Moore only complained like the rest of us about Mooney's dreadful writing. He and other anthropologists — including professor L. George Moses, notable for his biography of Mooney, and whom I had talked with once — had eked out their own transcriptions, but bypassed the six pages on the tipi hide tanning. Both Moore and Moses told me they knew nothing about tanning, and that those technical notes were irrelevant to their own interests and research on the man and the Southern Cheyenne. Moore did offer to put me in touch with his present day Cheyenne "informants," for which I thanked him with secreted skepticism.

Not one to be deterred, if others had endured Mooney's scribbles to illuminate the man's first hand encounters with the Southern Cheyenne — so would I. There was nothing left to do but to transcribe the notes myself, which took weeks, then months, to figure out, matching known letters to a very scant smattering of legible words. As I thought of it, I was creating a "Natural Tanners Mooney Rosetta Stone." Eventually, I cracked the Mooney Code. To the best of my knowledge it is the only such in-depth accounting of Indian tanning in the historical literature. I was astonished by the man's astute observations, if not his calligraphic impediments I had to fight my way through. To me, Mooney is an unknown and unsung hero in the natural tanning culture today, and to whom I am forever indebted. What I learned from him and those Indian women brought me ever closer to the truth about bison tanning. But there's more to this story. I still needed to put Mooney's notes to the reality of that hide tipi. I decided to fly to Chicago without an appointment, and, if necessary, steal my way into the bowels of the museum's air-conditioned catacomb of Indian artifacts. On the plane, I conjured various schemes to get past the sentinels I imagined guarding the entrances. This was a buckskin tanner's war, and I would breech the museum's defenses!

But when I got to the museum, thence to the Native American artifact department, which seemed rather dark and dreary, there was just one "guard," an anthropologist, and, I have to admit, a stunningly beautiful one. And I further confess, that, for a few minutes, I forgot about the tipi and directed my attentions to her alone. In my defense, I was single. Anyway, after much small talk she wanted to know what I was doing there. I can't remember to this day what I said, but when I was done, she said, "Well, I guess I can take you down there to see it." I think the cramped little elevator took us down seven stories underground, but I'm not sure, as I was overly excited (by the prospect of at long last seeing the tipi).

We walked down this long, seemingly endless aisle with what looked like locked wire cages on either side full of artifacts. We finally arrived at the tipi, which laid on the floor in its wide cage that couldn't have been much more than two foot high. She then said, "We can't bring it out, you'll have to examine it where it lies." I stooped down, and there it was. I could see that it had colorful designs painted on it. I reached in and took a section of it in hand. It was exactly as I expected. In less than a minute, I got up and said, "That's all I need to see." She gave me a puzzled look, and we returned to her office. Once there, she asked me what I thought, and would I be willing to look at other Indian tanned artifacts that were nearby. I agreed and I was taken to another room full of 19th century Native American garments of every sort. If the U.S. government took Indian lands, museums took their personal belongings. I bewildered her further by saying, "Nothing here was brain tanned by Indians, including the tipi down below." I returned home.

Breakthrough: Cheyenne women tanners and Mooney's Notes

After the visit to the Field Museum, I called John Moore to tell him that I cracked the "Mooney Code," and would no longer need the help of his Cheyenne contacts. Several months later, I wrote James Glenn to tell him the same and that I had successfully tanned a bison hide as a result. The path to this breakthrough was not easy, and required every bit of information I had gathered to date, and my many years of buckskin tanning to work past the many tanning myths that stood in the way.

Mooney's notes and photographs were revealing that the Southern Cheyenne tanners, 10 to 12 women, had a very precise method of producing pliable but "untanned" hides. They worked in teams and in shifts, day and night, often dealing with inclement weather, which held matters up repeatedly. Canopies of canvas were provided by Mooney to give them some shelter from the sun and rain as they worked. Hides were staked ("50 stakes per hide") on the ground to dry, flesh side down, and then scraped to remove the hair, which Mooney translated to mean "graining." They were removing the epidermis or "grain" of the hide, which won't surprise buckskin tanners today. But they also used "graining bones" to remove long strands of dermal fibers on the flesh side; hence, the term graining, as I read Mooney's notes, had a broader meaning to the Cheyenne women than just removing epidermis on the hair side. Here and there Mooney applied Cheyenne terms for tools and procedures, which I've omitted here as redundant to this discussion. As buckskin tanners, we just want to know what the women did — it ain't a course in speaking Cheyenne!

After graining, the hides were moistened with water to impart flexibility for the next step of the process. To my surprise, they splashed *hot water* over the hides, which the women told Mooney was the "old way," and the "best way" to work the hides! They also laid grass over the soaked hides to keep the moisture from evaporating. But their preference was to use soaking "tubs" that Mooney also provided. Next, by means of ropes, the soaked hides were hung from the neck and shoulders from a horizontal pole that was supported by two upright posts, which constituted a tanning frame, of which there were several. A hide was then loosely staked from the tail end and hips at an angle just above the ground; in effect, forming a slanted canopy of sorts. With scrapers, the women then defleshed the hides, again working in teams to relieve each other. There were many coordinated comings and goings from their tanning camp.

Next came their tanning "mash." Mooney supplied them with copious amounts of brains, liver, and lard, often leaving to get more at their request. The brains and livers were cooked separately for "one hour each," then the lard was added to produce "oil." Throughout the process, the moist and oiled hides were rubbed over sinew ropes, which they took from backs of the animals — apparently Mooney had them killed nearby. The sinew was then stretched out to dry on their tanning frames. Some of these ropes fell apart, the women complaining to Mooney that the sinew strands were "too short." They also rubbed hides over metal scythes. Like before, they rubbed the hides in teams of two, again relieving each other as the work was arduous. They also tied the hide to the tanning frame and twisted it with a stick to wring out moisture. Hides that threatened to harden up were moistened again by throwing more hot water over them as they lay on the ground, if, instead, they weren't returned to the preferred soaking tubs. The women struggled with getting the hides pliable, requesting more lard again and again, as the brain mixture wasn't enough ("not enough oil" they told Mooney) to do the job. Eventually, they finished all 27 hides and begin trimming and sewing 30 days after starting. To me, a remarkable feat.

Now that I knew what they had done, stepwise, and with what, you can appreciate why the trip to the Field Museum was crucial. You should be able to predict what I found at the museum: basically raw, un-tanned skins stitched together, that had been rendered sufficiently pliable by "stuffing" it with the oily mixture of brains, liver, and lots of lard. I had deduced that the ratio of these ingredients was important to the Cheyenne tanners. The whitish color of the tipi reflected the lard (rendered animal fat), brains, and to a lesser extent, the liver), all of which dried into the dermis of the tipi's hides. As noted, the women introduced their "mash" while hot into the raw skin. All of this made sense to me.

But what has not been discussed in the historical literature — as it pertains to tanning bison hides — is what follows the braining, and what would have happened to this one for a generation if, no doubt, the Cheyenne women had had their way.

Bison buckskin tanning

So, who on the planet today whose ever seen a movie about Indians on the Great Plains (e.g., Dances With Wolves) doesn't know what happens inside every tipi? *The Indians built fires in them.* We're talking heat and smoke: tanning aldehydes! And this is what's missing in the historical accounts of bison tanning.

Thinking a bit further about this, the fatty mash that tipi dwelling Indian tribes used would naturally repel rain, a necessity in any household shelter. But, as the heat warmed the mash — as the Cheyenne tanners demonstrated — the moistened reticulated fibers of the dermis naturally loosened, enabling the warm smoke to gradually penetrate and react chemically with the exposed fibers. Over time, the lubricated dermis comprising the conical walls of the tipi became increasingly tanned and darkened by the aldehyde enriched smoke. 19th century photographs of Plains Indian tipis are revealing of upper walls and smoke flaps nearly blackened by smoke. Eventually, tipi covers would be replaced and the older covers, now fully tanned, were washed and turned into garments and other items used in the daily lives of the people.

Before transporting the Cheyenne tipi to the St. Louis Exposition, Mooney invited others to see the tipi which the Cheyenne woman erected at the Darlington Indian Agency (Oklahoma Territory). A related incident involving "smoke" found its way into the April 13th, 1904 edition of the Chicago Daily News by a reporter who also came to see it:

"Professor Mooney permitted the tepee to be inspected by strangers for the first time on New Year's Day, and many handsome women and gold-braided officers came from the garrison at Fort Reno to see it. In spite of a roaring wind that came down from the north across the brown prairies they found the tepee surprisingly warm and comfortable. A small fire blazed cheerily in the hollow place scooped in the ground at the center, and the smoke went curling out at the opening at the top. White visitors stood around and sneezed and coughed and wiped involuntary tears from their cheeks, till Prof. Mooney said: 'Sit down on the seats and you will not be annoyed by the smoke.'"

Of course, "brain tan" buckskinners today all know that if you smoke the deerskin (softened by the brain mash), it will authentically tan, and dry relatively soft instead of rawhide, if it is soaked in water. The leap to a bison hide, however, isn't so easy. The Plains Indian way was as I explained. But this won't work if one is using the same mash and trying to make it soft and pliable like the deer buckskin. I proved that, but so have others. It can't happen because "brain tan" won't work on the tight, reticulated collagens of bison dermis, or other members of the bovine family. So what we see are brain tanners thinning down bison skins and robes to the epidermal layer. Get it thin enough, however, and the hide will weaken, rip, and require stitching to repair — and this is widely reported by brain tanners working buffalo skins today. Indian tanners were faced with the same problem. Either the robes were thinned down to the "tear point," or the robe wouldn't work for clothing. A rug maybe, but not clothes. Right? Maybe not.

At the Field Museum, we recall the anthropologist who asked me to look at other items purportedly tanned by 19th century Plains Indians. What I saw were robes and other items that were a mingling of brain-tanned in the pre-tanned sense, but also what looked like were aldehyde tanned, both often decorated with Indian paints, hair of some type, bead and quillwork. I suspected, at the time, the leather was either commercially tanned and brokered out to Indian women for decorating by "Indian traders" — known to be active among Plains Indians in the 19th century — then selling the goods to whites and museums as authentic Indian artifacts, or tanned by Indians using aldehydes in some form. Either seemed feasible to me as tanning and rendering plants had been set-up in Chicago, St. Louis and other locations not far from or along the edges of the still "wild" Great Plains. This was all part of the "Great Buffalo Trade" that contributed heavily to the species near extinction from 25 million to less than 600 individuals by 1890. Plains

Indians gathered at trading posts to obtain goods that they needed in exchange for what traders needed. Bison robes and other authentic "Indian made" items were in great demand by wealthy individuals, collectors, and museums. Conceivably, tanned hides, tanning ingredients, and other things crossed between traders and Indian women. Fish oils, by then widely available from commercial rendering plants, could have entered the trade. On these points, historians would be the right persons to explore the Great Buffalo Trade at this level of investigation. At museums and in private collections, purported Indian tanned artifacts would necessarily be subjected to DNA sequencing to ascertain what animal or plant substances were used. All of this is possible.

An experiment

The time had come by late 1983 to test my theory of tanning bison the "natural way." The Cheyenne tipi and Mooney's notes provided all the evidence one could possibly want to explain how bison hides "pre-tanned" would become aldehyde-tanned over time by virtue of the Indian's campfire culture inside their hide tipis. I decided to move on to the question, what would happen if other aldehydes were naturally available to the Indians. To me, it didn't matter what the source was, only whether it would work using a known Plains Indian method. By then I was not only familiar with what the Southern Cheyenne and their allies, the Arapaho, did, but also the Sioux through Larry Belitz's work. Fish oil seemed logical since it is commercially available now, and probably would have been indigenously so to the Plains Indians (and other tribes) in the 19th century and before.

Returning to my cabin for the last time, I obtained another bison hide, this time a bull hide I got from Larry and that I wasn't going to thin down at all. Why not? If it's going to tan out with my new mash, why bother thinning it at all? Either it's going to work or not. After all, what good would a thinned down bison hide do structurally for a 19th century tipi? In fact, I recall reading about one of the Cheyenne men attending Mooney's tipi "open house," complaining that the commercial cow hides available in Indian Territory were inferior to the "thick" hides they used during the Cheyenne's buffalo days. When I read that comment, I knew I was on the right track.

Here's what happened:

I split the hide down the center from head to tail cutting through the "hump," the thickest part of the hide (*facing page*), and split each half. Like the deer skin described in the previous chapter, I removed the hair in a lime solution, then de-limed it. Next, I framed one quarter (about the size of one deer skin), the one with half the hump, defleshed it, and let it dry out. Next, I "grained" off the epidermis. Then I soaked the hide (still in the frame) in the pond until saturated and pliable. Thick hides like this don't stretch out the same as deer due to dermal reticulation as explained earlier. Finally, I "stuffed" the hide over several soakings with brains, liver, and neat's-foot oil, until the hide was opaque and dried out in the hot sun. Basically, this brought the hide to the same place as the Cheyenne tipi hides, and what I do with deer skins. I decided to withhold the fish oil at this stage. Knowing from my previous failures that the hide would not soften out no matter how much I might rub it over a rope and knead it over my knee, the time had come to change course.

I soaked the framed (quarter) hide one last time in the pond to soften it. I gave it just one light scraping on each side to remove excess mash, and cut it from the frame. This quarter hide would be easy to handle and, if I was right, tan as readily as the entire hide the way I was going to do it.

I then prepared another mash of brains and liver, but replaced the neat's-foot oil with the fish oil. Like the Cheyenne tanners, I heated the mixture up until very warm and poured it into 5 gallon plastic bucket. I then added the bison square and stuck it in the mash, mixing it all up thoroughly. I even wrung the square out in there with my hands, and let it soak up the mash again. In my own way, this replicated what the Cheyenne did on their frames, except for the fish oil. I let the hide sit in the solution over night.

The next morning I hurried to the kitchen to check out the hide. It had changed. It had darkened considerably and looked more like smoked leather than raw skin. Very exciting — a positive indicator of aldehyde tannage! I decided to let it soak in the mash another night. The following morning, I removed it from the bucket, dumped the mash, and filled it with warm soapy water. I thoroughly and repeatedly washed the hide until clean. I wrung it out, and draped it over the side of the bucket. It was clearly no longer rawhide. Although still damp, it was completely tanned. I did nothing more but let it dry out. I then picked it up, stunned

(*Above*) Returning to my cabin, I obtained another bison hide, this time a bull hide that wasn't thinned at all.

(*Right*) I split the hide down the center from head to tail cutting through the 'hump,' the thickest part of the hide. I then cut the halves into quarters.

by the soft – but not stretchy – beautiful finish that never hit a rubbing rope! As expected, the leather had darkened a bit like smoke tan, although it was never smoked. I would describe the finish similar to a thick piece of felt and about as flexible, but denser, like smoked deer hide. You could make an array of clothing and other items from it as the Plains Indians would have using old, smoke tanned tipi hides. It was also strong and not given to any kind of tearing. And, in case you're wondering, no there wasn't any fishy smell either, then or now!

On the facing page, I've included a large swatch taken from the bison "quarter." It's the same piece, but flipped so you can see and compare the texture of the grain versus the flesh side. The piece is about ¼ inch thick. At the hump it is nearly ¾ inch thick! Once more, no part of the hide was subjected to rubbing.

I wrote Belitz immediately and included a sample swatch cut from the quarter. I also included a rough draft of my tanning manuscript, but didn't explain how I tanned the bison sample. His response was surprisingly reserved, "The bison remnant sent is very educational. You never explained what the hide was impregnated with. I'd be interested in knowing." I sent samples to others, too, but strangely, no one responded. I decided to "kill off the manuscript" I had written in 1979 prior to the bison hide experiment. It would have to be re-written.

By then, 1983, my wild horse research was altering my farrier career and I needed to deal with that, including writing my first book, *The Natural Horse: Lessons From the Wild*, which was published by Northland Publishing in 1992. It's now 40 years later, and following what has been a major shift in my professional work with horses to "Natural Hoof Care Practitioner," I finally found the time (barely) to write this book. My original research papers for this book date back to the late 1970s when I first visited the Western History Collections. I have somehow managed to keep all my letters, images, documents, and leather samples in one box for all these years. A miracle since, being nomadic for most of my life, I've moved so many times since the 70s and I can't even recall where the box was kept most of the time if my life depended on it!

Carry on fellow buckskin tanners!

Postscript

For me, the long journey of discovery and my mission to share what I learned has come to an end. Others will have to pick up the ball and run with it as I pass deeper into the uncertainties that come with what society deems "old age." I am eternally grateful to the string of people who made my quest possible, including those whom I never shared a direct word or moment with, by letter or *vis á vis*. Such as James Mooney. It appears that Mooney passed on the only step by step accounting of Indian tanning the "old way" with a result we can see and touch 115 years later. Remarkable. His life story is equally remarkable, and I encourage my readers to read Mooney's bio by L.G. Moses, *Indian Man: A Biography of James Mooney*. (2002, University of Nebraska Press). And, of course, there are the Cheyenne Indian women who agreed to help Mooney save an integral part of the Cheyenne cultural way, in fact, of the Plains Indian way as I understand it now.

At the time, Mooney and the Cheyenne people were both struggling with forces that threatened the project. In Washington, DC, congressional leaders were doubting the value of works like Mooney's at the BAE, even his credibility as a scientist. Even the BAE itself! The attitude was, if not of practical value, then it is not relevant. Not long before Mooney's arrival in Oklahoma Territory, the Cheyenne had been driven from their homeland on the Great Plains by the U.S. military and settlers wanting their land. The entire Cheyenne nation was relocated — and not without subjecting them to the worst violence imaginable — to Indian Territory created by congress in what would soon become the State of Oklahoma, where the Chicago Daily News reporter noted with remorse, "the Indians grow poorer as the moons ride to the west."

Today, legions of buckskin tanners from many different interests and disciplines carry on the "old way" of Indians, trappers, explorers, and even the traders I mentioned earlier. I've asked myself, why is this so? What is this bygone connection to the frontier past? Why tan a hide the old way? For me, it's a very "unadulterated" connection to nature, and to people who once lived closely to the land in ways that are not likely to happen ever again. On another level, just seeing and feeling the miraculous transition of rawhide to leather in one's hands is enough. And knowing too, we hope, that there is a recognition that the animal that gave of itself to us was not for nothing.

Chemistry of Buckskin Tanning[1]
by Jaime Jackson

For years, I have marveled at the properties of "brain tan" leather. How is it that this beautiful, white, velvety soft leather, when soaked in water dries to rawhide hardness? Yet, the same piece of white leather, first smoked over a smudge fire, then soaked in water will dry soft? What role do the brains play in tanning and does smoke actually chemically alter the white tanned leather (as Catlin suggests[2])?

To answer these questions, I once again refer to the literature, and in addition, to my own experience as well as the tanning industry where applicable.

Definition of tanning and the histology of skin

Originally, tanning (from the Latin word for oak bark) was applied to describe the process of converting the putrescible skin into the stable product leather. We can more easily understand the chemical transformations that occur during the production of leather, if we first take a (very) brief look at the histology of animal skin. Then we can identify the principal chemical structures found in skin which undergo macromolecular reorganization during tanning.

Integument, or skin,[3] can readily be described in terms of a cross-sectional

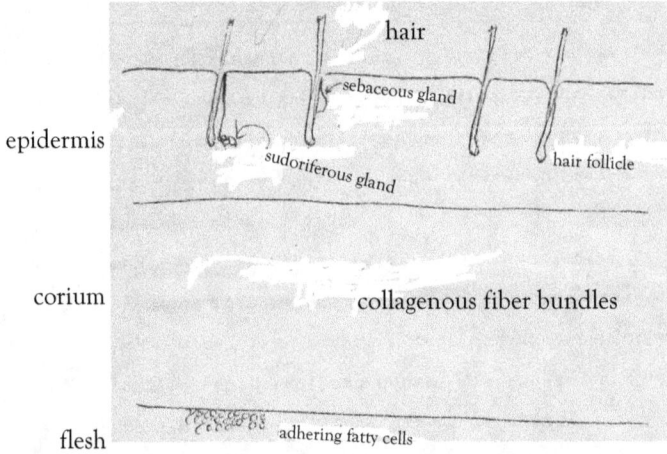

[1] Written in 1979 by Jaime Jackson. Edited by Jean J. Tancous, Tanners Council Laboratory of America, University of Cincinnati, Ohio. Excuse the poor quality of line drawings, I scanned these from the original manuscript.

[2] Catlin, G. *Letters and Notes On the Manners, Customs, and Conditions of North American Indians*, 2 vol., NY, Dover Publications, Inc., VI, p. 45 (1973).

[3] In this text the word skin refers primarily to integument. However, when we are talking about the skin that is removed from an animal's carcass, some confusion may arise. The following quotation, taken from a leather source book by the New England Tanners Club explains: "By convention, the tanner usually refers to the skin coverings of large animals (cows, steers, horses, buffaloes, etc.) as 'hides.' Those of smaller animals (calves, sheep, goats, pigs, etc.) are called 'skins.'" *Leather Facts*, PO Box 371, Peabody, Massachusetts, 01960. 6 (1965).

schematic:

From a histological standpoint, adhering flesh is not considered as part of the skin; in fact, during tanning it is removed as much as possible. Flesh is composed of varying amounts of fatty adipose tissue, blood vessels, nerves, and voluntary muscle.

This leaves us with the epidermis and corium (dermis). In the production of buckskin, the epidermis is removed; while in robe tanning (fur intact) it remains. Since both areas are chemically altered during tanning, a brief discussion of each is in order.

The epidermal area is that portion of the fresh skin or hide which contains the hair, the fair follicles, the epidermis and its appendages (various glands and supportive protein fiber bundles). The epidermis itself is said to be stratified since it is composed of four layers — collectively referred to as the epithelium.

The corium is the main portion of the skin and is largely responsible for many of the characteristics of the finished leather. It is composed of collagenous fiber bundles which hold in their interspaces reticular tissue fibers, fibroblasts, blood vessels and nerve tissue.

Generally, the structures (e.g., fiber bundles, blood vessels, etc.) found in both the corium and epidermal area are similar in character; however, they are usually larger in the corium. Also, epidermal and dermal fiber bundles vary in density and layer thickness from animal to animal.

Approximately 80 percent of the dry matter of skin is made up of complex nitrogenous organic compounds known as proteins. All proteins belong to one of two large groups: the fibrous proteins and globular proteins. Both types are found in the skin. Fiber bundles constitute the main portion of skin and are classified as fibrous proteins, or collagens. These proteins react with the tanning agents to produce leather. The globular proteins are water soluble and are therefore removed partially during the early, soaking stages of tanning.

The point I wish to emphasize here is that proteins, or collagens since we are talking about skin tissue, are the basis for tannage. We might therefore define leather then as collagens in the tanned state.

There are many different tanning agents available to alter the chemical structures of collagens. In fact, these agents do not form a distinct class of chemical compounds, As examples, there are the chromium salts, vegetable tannins, aldehydes, syntans, and unsaturated oils. Basically, however, tanning agents will fall into two classes: (1) mineral tanning agents and (2) tanning agents of organic nature. For our purposes, we will focus attention upon unsaturated oil tanning since the application of brains (Class 2) involves an unsaturated animal oil as the tanning agent.

Oil tannage or Chamois

Oil tanning produces a leather having characteristics quite different from all other types of tanning. Such leather is as soft as cloth, is smooth and very stretchy. It takes up water like a sponge, but gives it up again just as easily. As well, this leather can also readily absorb grease.

The use of unsaturated oils for tanning leather and furs has been practiced since prehistoric times — and was not limited to the Indians of North America. Originally, the pelts of wild animals, especially chamois, deer, elk, antelope, etc., were used for oil tanning. Oil tanned leather is also called chamois (after the goatlike antelope whose hides were tanned by the French and Swiss). Chamois, today, is commercially prepared from the corium portion of Merino sheepskins.

Basically, all types of light and loose-textured skins can be worked into chamois leather (heavier, more coarsely textured hides such as buffalo were tanning by the American Indians using chamois techniques; of course, such large hides did not have the same softness as smaller, light skins).

Today, chamois leather is produced by the tanning industry. Cod-liver oil or seal oil is the tanning agent. It is helpful to understand the theory of fish-oil tanning, since the chemistry of the process has been investigated by the industry and explains, for the most part, the chemistry of brain tanning.

Fish-oil tanning

Several tanning effects are involved in chamois (fish-oil) tannage. One originates from the aldehydes formed during heat-drying after the oil is stuffed into the skin and undergoes oxidation by the atmosphere. Another comes from the formation of tanning peroxides in the oil during the heating stage. And the last effect apparently involves an adsorption with no direct chemical combination between hide and fish-oil oxidation products occurring.

Investigators have long known that aldehydes are formed during the oxidative decomposition (rancidification) of unsaturated fats and oils.[1] The characteristic pungent odor of acolein has been noted in the thermal decomposition (autoxidation) of fish oil during tanning. Proctor notably was the first to express the possibility of acrolein. tannage, believing that this arose out of glycerides found in the fish oil.[2] However, Wood showed that good chamois leather could be produced from the free fatty acids of the oil instead of the oil itself.[3] Salway then proved that acrolein is formed from the free fatty acids of linseed oil during autoxidation fo the follwong scheme of reaction[4]:

$$R\text{--}CH=CH\text{--}CH=CH\text{--}CH=CH\text{--}R_1$$
$$\downarrow$$
$$R\text{--}\underset{\underset{O\text{---}O}{|}}{CH}\text{--}\underset{|}{CH}\text{--}CH=CH\text{--}\underset{\underset{O\text{---}O}{|}}{CH}\text{--}\underset{|}{CH}\text{--}R_1$$
$$\downarrow$$
$$R\cdot CHO + CHO\cdot CH=CH\cdot CHO + CHO\cdot R_1$$
$$\text{Fumeric dialdehyde}$$
$$\downarrow$$
$$CH_2=CH\cdot CHO + CO \quad HOCO\cdot CH=CH\cdot CHO$$
$$\text{Acrolein} \qquad\qquad\qquad \downarrow$$
$$\qquad\qquad\qquad\qquad\qquad CH_2=CH\cdot CHO + CO_2$$

Other tanning aldehydes have been shown to occur during oxidative fish-oil decomposition. Some of these are simple, short-chained dialdehydes such as glyoxal.[5] Others are unsaturated aldehyde acids (of relatively low molecular weight) in a mixture of aldehydes.[6]

The aldehyde group (–CHO) is extremely reactive. the nature of the radical in the general formula for aldehydes (R–CHO) determines the kind and extent of reactivity towards the amino acids, polypeptides, and proteins found in skin. For example, aldehydes react with amino (–NH$_2$) groups in the fibers of the dermal network in a cross-linking manner:

$$\text{--}NH_2 + 2R\cdot CHO + NH_2\text{--}$$
$$\downarrow$$
$$\text{--}NH\text{--}O\text{--}\underset{\underset{R}{|}}{\overset{\overset{H}{|}}{C}}\text{--}\underset{\underset{R}{|}}{\overset{\overset{H}{|}}{C}}\text{--}NH\text{--} + HOH$$

[1]Taufel, K., *Fette u. Seifen.* 50. p. 387 (1943).
[2]Proctor, H.R., *Principles of Leather Manufacture*, 2nd ed., Princeton, N.F., D. Van Nostrand Co., (1922).
[3]Wood, J.T., quoted by Proctor, H.R. Reference 46, p. 461.
[4]Salway, A.H., *Journal of Chemical Society*, 109, p. 138 (1919).
[5]Kuntzel, A., and Nungesser, T., *Leder.* 7, p. 115 (1956).
[6]Danby, J.P., Dissertation, Leeds University (1951).

Another important part of the aldehyde tanning process is that fish-oil aldehydes do not tan well during an acid reaction.[1] The hide or skin must be washed in a 1 to 2 percent soda solution repeatedly, to induce an alkaline reaction. Apparently, the acidity exists after the autoxidation of the fish-oils, because of the organic acids formed.

According to Fahrion, in the first phase of tanning, cyclic perioxides of fatty acids arise from the oxidation of the fish oil[2]:

$$R-CH=CH-R-CH=CH-R + 2O_2 \rightarrow R-CH-CH-R-CH-CH-R$$
$$\,||||$$
$$\,O-OO-O$$

A part of this molecule then reacts with the amino groups of the skin according to this scheme:

$$R-CH-CH-R-CH-CH-R$$
$$||||$$
$$OHOHOO$$
$$\phantom{R-OHOH}||$$
$$\phantom{R-OHOH}NHNH$$
$$\boxed{SKIN}$$

Other investigators have propose different hypotheses for the direct union of fish-oil with the hide substance. Mathur and Li hold that hydroxy groups are the reactive units with the amino groups.[3,4] Pederson and Glavind claim that the oxidized fatty acids first react with the carboxyl groups of the collagen like an ester[5]:

$$R-CH-CH=CH-R + P-COOH \rightarrow R-CH-CH-R + H_2O$$

with H hydroperoxide and collagen P.

[1] Czepelak, V., Anniversary Number, *Osterr. Leder-z.* zum Wiener Kongress fur Gerbereichemie und Ledertechnik., Wien, (1954).
[2] Fahrion, W. A., *Angew. Chem.*, 16, p. 665 (1903).
[3] Mathur, B.N., *J. Am. Leather Chemists' Assoc.*, 22, p. 2 (1927).
[4] Lio, Y.H., *J. Am. Leather Chemist Assoc.*, 77, p. 380 (1927).
[5] Pedersen, J.W., and Glavind, J., *Aeta Chem. Scand.*, 6, p. 451 (1952); 6, p. 453 (1927).

The resulting epoxide then cross-links between two collagen molecules by reacting with another carboxyl group:

$$R\text{--}CH\text{--}\overset{O}{\overset{\diagup\diagdown}{CH\text{--}CH}}\text{--}R + P\text{--}COOH \rightarrow R\text{--}CH\text{--}\overset{\overset{P}{|}}{\underset{|}{\overset{O=C}{|}}}\text{--}CH\text{--}R$$

$$\text{collagen}$$

The last probable tanning effect involves the adsorption of polymerization products of oxidized fish-oil or fish-oil fatty acids. Here, there is no direct chemical reaction with the hide. the polymerizates exist in the oil in colloidal dispersion and are adsorbed by the hide. The resulting "film" surrounds the skin fibers and remains in the leather after removal of the excess fish oil during the tanning process. The oil film gives the characteristic color — yellow to yellow-brown — to chamois leather.[1]

Brain tanning

Skins or hides stuffed with brain matter and rubbed mechanically until dry are white to cream-colored, extremely supple, stetchy and readily take up water like a sponge. There, the similarities with chamois (fish-oil) leather come to an end. As mentioned previously, the skin stuffed with brain matter will revert to rawhide upon drying (unless simultaneously rubbed). Clearly, the collagens are not tanned and the reasons for this are evident from the previous discussion of fish-oil tannage.

The most obvious reason lies in the color of the leather itself: untanned collagens are white (i.e., give a white skin). The fact that some brain tannage is yellowish indicates that probably some atmospheric oxidation occurs along the double bonds of the oils:

$$\text{--}\underset{H}{C}=\underset{H}{C}\text{--} + O_2 \rightarrow \text{--}\underset{\underset{O\text{---}O}{|}}{CH}\text{--}\underset{|}{CH}\text{--}$$

---

[1]Chambard, P., and Michallet, L., *J. Soc. Leather Trade Che.*, 11, p. 559 (1927).

It is improbable that any significant degree of polymerization occurs as a result of thermal decomposition during autoxidation. In fish-oil tanning, the polymers coat the fiber structure by adsorption imparting a hydrophobic quality. This is not characteristic of the white leather, since water is not easily relinquished by the still hydrophilic collagens during the drying phase.

The last reason is the lack of aldehyde reaction. If the white leather is washed repeatedly in a warm soda bath, it will still dry hard and tinny (into rawhide). this can be explained by the special chemical composition of fish oils within the natural triglycerides.

Vegetable fats and land-animal oils contain mainly fatty acids with 16 or 18 carbon atoms. Among the unsaturated fatty acids occurring the number of double bonds is limited to 1, 2 or 3. Higher unsaturated fatty acids are, for all practical purposes, just not there. In marine oils, on the other hand, the picture is altogether different. Fatty acids with long chains (20, 22 and 24 carbon atoms) with unsaturated double bonds (containing as many as 6 double bonds per fatty acid residue) are numerous. Therefore, the brains inherently lack the necessary unsaturated fatty acids that in turn make the formation of tanning aldehydes probable.

Smoke tanning

As we know, American Indians smoked their skins and hides to protect them from moisture. Smoke contains aldehydes such as acrolein, acetaldehyde, and formaldehyde, all of which have known tanning capacities. The heat from the fire aids in the oxidation of the brain oil to promote further, although negligent, aldehyde and polymer production.

Summary

Clearly, the Indian obtained no chemical tannage of the collagens with braining. But it makes sense that they would first lubricate their skins and hides with aqueous emulsions of fats (complex lipids): the skins had to be manually rubbed to achieve softness, and the brains (through lubrication of the fibers) made the job easier. To protect their leather products from water damage, the Indians smoked their skins thoroughly over warm smudge fires.

Source Material[1]

Barnett, H.G. *The Coastal Salish of British Columbia.* Eugene: University of Oregon. p. 124-125 (1928).

Bushneth, D. see Hodge, #8, p. 593.

Catlin, G. *Letters and Notes On the Manners, Customs, and Conditions of North American Indians,* 2 vol., NY, Dover Publications, Inc., VI, p. 45 (1973).

Fletcher, A.C. *The Omaha Tribe.* Lincoln: University of Nebraska Press (1911).

Gunther, E. *Klallam Ethnography.* Seattle: University of Washington Press. p. 219 (1927).

Hodge, F. *The Handbook of American Indians North of Mexico.* p. 591-593.

Laubin, R. & G. *The Indian Tipi.* Norman: University of Oklahoma Press. p. 88 (1977).

Lawson. See Hodge, #8, p. 593.

Lowie, R.H. *The Crow Indians.* New York: Rinehart & Company. p. 77 (1935).

Lyford, C. *Quill and Beadwork of the Western Sioux.* U.S. Department of the Interior. Haskell Institute Print Department. Kansas. p. 33-37 (1940).

Mooney, J. *Miscellaneous Notes On the Cheyenne.* 6 pp. describing hide tanning for replica of "Bushyhead Tipi." Transcribed by Jaime Jackson (1979).[2]

Schoolcraft. See Hodge: #8, *Narrative Journal.* p. 323. (1821).

Schulz, G.W. *Blackfeet and Buffalo.* University of Oklahoma. p. 32-33 (1962).

Solomon, J.H. *Book of Indian Crafts and Indian Lore.* New York: Harper & Brothers. p. 103-105 (1928).

---

[1]This is a small sampling of sources I accessed. I picked these because the authors observations were made among the Indian people they visited either before or during the early reservation days in the U.S. I was less interested in later observers or "second hand accounts." Some source material is include in the text of this book, but omitted here. As I wrote early in the book, *Buckskin Tanner* is not an academic treatise on American Indian tanning, but a useful guide to natural tanning.

[2]Transcription available for purchase at http://www.NaturalWorldPublications.net

Image Attributions

Cover (front)
- Tommie Stevens*

Cover (back)
- Above: Jaime Jackson
- Below: Jill Willis

Title page
- Tommie Stevens

P.3 (facing page)
- From the collection of daveland-web.com

P. 5
- Above: Unknown
- Below: Ron Colgna

P. 7
- Western History Collections, University of Oklahoma Library.

P. 8
- Western History Collections, University of Oklahoma Library.

P. 14
- Norm Kidder, Coyote Hills Regional Park, 8000 Patterson Ranch Rd, Fremont, CA 94555

P. 17
- Jaime Jackson

P. 18
- Tommie Stevens (Jasper, AR)

P. 19
- Jaime Jackson

P. 20, 22-25, 27-34
- Tommie Stevens

P. 37
- Jaime Jackson

P. 38
- Henry L. Batterman Fund and the Frank Sherman Benson Fund - Brooklyn Museum

P. 45
- Diego Delso: Field Museum, Chicago, Illinois, USA

P. 55
- Tommie Stevens

P. 57
- Jaime Jackson

P. 70
- Above: Jill Willis
- Below: Unknown

*Tommie was a client of mine and a friend. Fiercely independent, she lived on her land in the mountains not far from me, with a couple of horses that I trimmed, and a ton of other animals including too many cats. Dinner meant waiting for her to catch a chicken, process it on the spot, cook it, and serve with other things out of her garden. She took an interest in my tanning and offered to photograph the process. Weren't for her, this book would have been impossible to do the way I wanted it, showing what happened over 40 years ago as part of my lifestyle — not staged today out of that context. A heavy smoker, Tommie died of lung cancer a few years later.

Index of Tanning Steps

The steps (Deer family):

Salt the hide, 11

Remove the hair, 11

De-lime the hide, 13

Make your scraping tool, 15

Make your stretching frame, 14

Lace the hide onto your frame, 16

Raise and secure the frame, 19

De-flesh the hide, 19

Remove the grain (epidermis), 21

Soak the hide in water, 22

Prepare your pre-tanning ingredients, 22

Add pre-tanning ingredients to skin, 24

Add more pre-tanning ingredients, 24

Remove hide from the frame, 26

Rub the skin into buckskin, 28

Stretch the buckskin in the finishing frame, 33

The steps (Bison):

Tanners Council Laboratory, University of Cincinnati, 39

Western History Collection, University of Oklahoma, 40

Union Hide - Oakland, California, 43

Chicago Field Museum, 44

Breakthrough: Cheyenne women tanners and Mooney's Notes, 47

Bison buckskin tanning, 49

An experiment, 51

About the Author

I've always been a maverick thinker and doer, never satisfied with life's limits as I've perceived them to be in the mainstream. For example, after leaving the U.S. Army in early 1970 with an honorable discharge, I joined other veterans in the antiwar movement in protest of the corporate "war for profits" in Vietnam and the average American's unwitting complicity. "No business as usual" was our mantra, and on many fronts the burgeoning protest movement confronted every institution across the country. As mounting numbers of dead and wounded were returned home, the entire nation began questioning and then demanding an end to the war. In 1975 President Nixon felt the hand of the movement and shut it down — the greatest military blunder in the history of the U.S. After that, we all went own separate ways.

My calling became "nature" and what we can learn as a species from our natural world, past and present. My books continue to tell my own story, where I've gone, what I've got myself into, with whom, and why. *Buckskin Tanner* is one chapter in that story.

Buckskin tanner, then and now . . .

www.ingramcontent.com/pod-product-compliance
Lightning Source LLC
Chambersburg PA
CBHW060501010526
44118CB00018B/2496